DYSLEXIA AN
EMPLOYM

DYSLEXIA AND EMPLOYMENT

A GUIDE FOR ASSESSORS, TRAINERS AND MANAGERS

EDITED BY SYLVIA MOODY

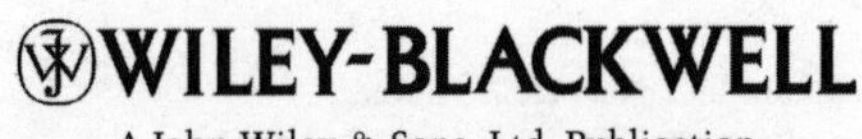

A John Wiley & Sons, Ltd, Publication

This edition first published 2009
© 2009 John Wiley & Sons, Ltd, except for pages 217-221 © Sylvia Moody and page 222 © Melanie Jameson.

Registered office
John Wiley & Sons, Ltd, The Atrium, Southern Gate, Chichester, West Sussex, PO19 8SQ, United Kingdom

For details of our global editorial offices, for customer services and for information about how to apply for permission to reuse the copyright material in this book please see our website at www.wiley.com.

The right of the editor to be identified as the author of the editorial material in this work has been asserted in accordance with the Copyright, Designs and Patents Act 1988.

All rights reserved. No part of this publication may be reproduced, stored in a retrieval system, or transmitted, in any form or by any means, electronic, mechanical, photocopying, recording or otherwise, except as permitted by the UK Copyright, Designs and Patents Act 1988, without the prior permission of the publisher.

Wiley also publishes its books in a variety of electronic formats. Some content that appears in print may not be available in electronic books.

Designations used by companies to distinguish their products are often claimed as trademarks. All brand names and product names used in this book are trade names, service marks, trademarks or registered trademarks of their respective owners. The publisher is not associated with any product or vendor mentioned in this book. This publication is designed to provide accurate and authoritative information in regard to the subject matter covered. It is sold on the understanding that the publisher is not engaged in rendering professional services. If professional advice or other expert assistance is required, the services of a competent professional should be sought.

Library of Congress Cataloging-in-Publication Data has been applied for

A catalogue record for this book is available from the British Library.

ISBN: 978-0-470-74090-3 (hbk)

ISBN: 978-0-470-69478-7 (pbk)

Set in 11.5/13.5pt Times by Aptara Inc., New Delhi, India
Printed in Singapore by Utopia Press Pte Ltd

Contents

The chapters are listed twice: (a) chronologically *below*
(b) by category *page ix*

Contents (by chapter category)

Introduction

Sylvia Moody

In recent years there has been a growing awareness of dyslexic difficulties in the workplace. Increasingly dyslexic employees are coming forward to seek assessment and support, and employers are becoming more aware of their obligations under the Disability Discrimination Act (DDA) to make reasonable adjustments for dyslexic difficulties. Consequently, dyslexia professionals are increasingly being asked to act as workplace dyslexia consultants.

Differences between Workplace and Educational Consultancy

The provision of assessment and training in a workplace context differs markedly from such provision in the educational sphere. In the educational sphere, the dyslexia consultant will deal mainly with other professional groups who are knowledgeable about dyslexia – educational psychologists, dyslexia tutors, dyslexia coordinators in schools and colleges.

By contrast, in the workplace the consultant usually has to liaise with, and give advice to, professional groups who have little or no knowledge of dyslexia – for example, Human Resources managers, line managers, Occupational Health advisors, training managers, union representatives, and lawyers. The consultant, therefore, has a duty to inform as well as to advise – and, in cases where disputes arise about

Dyslexia and Employment Edited by Sylvia Moody
© 2009 John Wiley & Sons, Ltd

reasonable adjustments, to engage in discussion or negotiation with the interested parties to try to resolve the situation.

A second difference between the educational and occupational spheres is that, in the former, diagnostic and needs assessments are usually done by two different people, while in the latter, both assessments are (ideally) carried out by the same assessor. The assessor may also subsequently carry out the workplace skills training.

Purpose of this Book

Few books are available at present on the subject of dyslexia in the workplace. Those that have been published (see Appendix IV) provide basic information on topics such as the nature of dyslexic difficulties, how these difficulties affect workplace efficiency, and how an employer can give help and support. This present book also provides such information, but it goes farther than this: it looks in detail at specific issues – tricky issues – which can arise in a workplace dyslexia consultancy, and at how these issues might be addressed and resolved. It also provides a guide to good practice in workplace needs and legal assessments and in skills training.

The Authors of the Book

This book is written by a group of dyslexia experts who specialize in workplace consultancy. They have extensive experience of assessing and training dyslexic employees, and of advising employers on how they can provide dyslexia support in accordance with the requirements of the DDA. They also have experience of acting as expert witnesses in employment tribunals.

What is dyslexia?

Before previewing the content of the chapters in this book, I shall pause for a moment to consider the meaning of the term 'dyslexia', or at least the meaning it has for the authors of this book. I shall also describe a related syndrome known as 'dyspraxia'.

Researchers are not agreed on a precise *definition* of dyslexia. The prevailing view is that dyslexia has its root in phonological difficulties, that is, difficulties with processing speech sounds. Difficulties with memory and/or perception are also 'in the frame'. In practice, however, the term 'dyslexia' is generally used more loosely to *describe* a number of difficulties which commonly co-occur. For the purposes of this book, a descriptive 'definition' of this sort suffices – and probably few people would argue with the following description:

Dyslexia is characterized by weaknesses in short-term memory, sequencing skills, and phonology. It affects not just word reading and spelling, but also higher level literacy skills such as reading for comprehension, notetaking, and structuring written work. In adults, difficulties with literacy skills may sometimes be subtle and difficult to spot. For example, a dyslexic adult may read and write with reasonable accuracy, but be exceptionally slow in carrying out these activities.

As well as literacy problems, there are often also difficulties with listening and speaking skills, and with organizing daily life and work/study schedules. Intellectual ability and creativity are not impaired.

What is dyspraxia?

The term 'dyspraxia' is used in the educational world to mean difficulties with physical coordination, spatial judgement, organizational skills, and social skills. There is a wide overlap between dyslexia and dyspraxia, and people with an interest in either or both of these syndromes should find this book useful.

The Contents of the Book

The book is a mixture of information, advice, discussion, and illustrative case studies. It contains four different types of chapter:

'Professional dilemma' chapters: 1, 4, 7, 11.

These chapters present major case studies illustrating particular issues which have arisen in our practice as workplace dyslexia consultants. Chapter 1, written by Sylvia Moody, focuses on the problem of disentangling dyslexic difficulties from difficulties of a more general nature, and deciding what level of support is appropriate for each. In Chapter 4, Pauline Sumner addresses concerns about employing dyslexic people in 'front line' professions, such as nursing and the fire service, and advises on measures that can be taken to minimize risk.

In Chapter 7, Katherine Kindersley describes how difficulties and disputes can arise in the workplace as a result of a change of manager or job requirements, and how a consultant might try to resolve such disputes. Finally, in Chapter 11, Melanie Jameson writes about the ways in which dyslexic difficulties can have an impact in the court room, and considers how members of the police service and the legal profession can be made more aware of the support that dyslexic people need during the judicial process.

Our aim in reporting these case studies is not to 'pronounce' on the best way that various conflicts might be resolved, but rather to present the solutions we found in particular cases and to offer these as the starting point for discussion.

'General perspective' chapters: 2, 5, 8, 10.

These four chapters look at the subject of dyslexia in the workplace from a more general perspective. Chapter 2 is a transcript of an interview with Brian Hagan – now a dyslexia consultant, but previously a Human Resources manager – in which he looks at dyslexia from the perspective of the HR department. In Chapter 5, Sarah Howard considers dyspraxic difficulties in the workplace. She reflects on ways in which managers can often be baffled by such difficulties (which are often more subtle than dyslexic ones), and gives advice on appropriate help and support.

Chapter 8 introduces the perspective of a dyslexic employee, Jeffrey, an engineer in a large telecommunications company. Jeffrey describes his difficult early years when he felt embarrassed about his difficulties, and the sometimes painful process of getting them recognized and accepted – by himself and others. He charts his progress from being a withdrawn person with a guilty secret to becoming an articulate public advocate for dyslexic people in the workplace.

In Chapter 10, Diana Bartlett considers the wide range of negative emotions that dyslexic people can feel, and how these interfere with both work efficiency and interactions with colleagues and managers.

'How to do it right' chapters: 3, 6, 9, 12.

These four chapters respectively give advice on

- how to do a Workplace Needs assessment;
- how to do an Assistive Technology assessment;
- how to set up a workplace skills training programme;
- how to write a legal report.

The chapters have a twofold purpose: to give guidance to dyslexia professionals who want to develop skills in workplace consultancy; and to give employers criteria for judging the quality of service they receive from workplace dyslexia consultants.

'Information points'

Interspersed among the main chapters are a series of 'Information points'. These are brief chapters – the equivalent of information sheets – and cover the following topics:

A. Dyslexic difficulties in the workplace.
B. Reasonable adjustments.
C. Disclosure guidelines.
D. Neurodiversity.
E. Visual stress.
F. Access to Work disability support.
G. Careers for dyslexic adults.
H. Disability discrimination legislation.
I. Specific learning difficulties: guidelines for lawyers.

Terminology

Dyslexia is constantly in danger of being 'medicalized'. It is often referred to as a 'condition' which somebody 'has' and which can be 'diagnosed'. It is described as being on a continuum with other syndromes which have the term 'deficit', or 'disorder' in their names. In an attempt to avoid this medicalizing tendency, a social model of disability has been developed which uses the vocabulary of 'difference' rather than difficulty. So a 'specific learning difficulty' becomes a 'specific learning difference'.

This approach has the advantage of presenting a more positive view of difficulties of various sorts by pointing up the variety of learning styles and coping strategies by which people can compensate for them. However, it can throw up some challenges. For example, could a dyspraxic person who constantly walks into doors and falls over usefully be described as a person with a 'walking difference'?

In this book, we have not espoused any particular model of disability – we have on the whole gravitated towards the everyday vocabulary we use in our practice, that is, we talk in terms of strengths, difficulties, and coping strategies, as we find this is something to which our clients can easily relate. However, the vocabulary of 'difference' has sometimes been used, as has the occasional medical term (e.g. diagnosis) in the interests of succinctness.

Conclusion

It is hoped that this book – with its mixture of information, personal experience, and discussion – will be of interest and use to dyslexia experts who are involved in workplace consultancy; and also to managers and other professional groups in the workplace who wish to become informed about good practice in supporting dyslexic employees.

Sylvia Moody
Dyslexia Assessment Service
London

CHAPTER 1

Dyslexia: A Case of Mistaken Identity?

Sylvia Moody

At first sight, the term 'dyslexia' appears reassuringly solid – a definite no-nonsense sort of word, denoting a precise condition. However, a glance below the surface reveals a very different picture: a confusing mix of contradictions, fuzzy concepts, blurred boundaries, disputed territories – as well as an admixture of some potentially explosive political agendas.

Whereas a person suffering from, say, measles will be given a diagnosis and treatment advice upon which all competent doctors will agree, a person presenting with what they suspect to be dyslexia may find that the professionals they consult will disagree both on the nature of their condition and on the best way to manage it.

In this chapter, as throughout the book, the use of technical jargon will be avoided, so that those of our readers who are not experts in dyslexia will be able to follow all the arguments and discussion presented here.

In the introduction to this book (page 3), I gave a general description of dyslexia which I believe to be uncontroversial. Beyond this description, however, dyslexia assessors need some definite criteria on the basis of which they can confidently identify or 'diagnose' dyslexia. (For a note on the use of medical terminology, see page 5.) The description I gave in the introduction could apply not just to people who have a specific learning difficulty (the usual view of dyslexia), but also to

Dyslexia and Employment Edited by Sylvia Moody
© 2009 John Wiley & Sons, Ltd

people whose abilities are generally in the low- or below-average range, in which case specific difficulties with, say, literacy or memory, may not stand out in contrast to intellectual or other strengths.

Some dyslexia experts argue that it is unhelpful to make a distinction between specific learning difficulties, such as dyslexia, and a more general picture of below-average abilities: they take the view that anyone who has literacy difficulties for *any* reason (e.g. low intellectual ability, lack of education) should be called dyslexic. Others stand this argument on its head, maintaining that no one should be called dyslexic because the word is so vague as to be meaningless. Proponents of this latter view, however, are often prepared to accept the term 'specific learning difficulties' – with the proviso that these difficulties should always be described in detail, and with the caveat that any sort of learning difficulty is on a continuum of difficulties, and so there will always be borderline cases. Most assessors of dyslexic adults steer a course somewhere midway between these two positions.

Assessors who have elected, perhaps with inner reservations, to use the word 'dyslexia' to denote a certain type of specific learning difficulty need to decide what criteria they will use to identify it. But here again is rich ground for controversy.

In the following two sections, I shall first give information about the different sorts of criteria that assessors use, and then present a case study which illustrates the problems which can occur if a wrong diagnosis is given. (In this chapter, feminine pronouns refer to the assessor, masculine pronouns to the client.)

Defining Dyslexia

Decades ago when specific difficulties with literacy first began to be recognized, and were given the name 'dyslexia', the diagnostic criterion in universal use was a significant discrepancy between IQ ('intelligence') and literacy skills.

The IQ–literacy discrepancy criterion for identifying dyslexia has held sway for a long time, and is still widely used. However, there are at least three reasons why this criterion may not be useful:

1. Much recent research has thrown doubt on there being a significant correlation between IQ and literacy. In other words, the doubters are

saying that knowing a person's IQ does not allow us to predict what his reading age is likely to be.

2. Since, as noted below, an IQ test measures a wide variety of cognitive abilities, it is not meaningful to compare literacy skills with the overall IQ score. In general, it is felt more useful to compare literacy with the section of the IQ test which covers verbal reasoning, vocabulary, and general knowledge. For the sake of simplicity in this chapter, I shall 'pare this section down' to verbal reasoning alone.
3. When we come to literacy, there is an even greater problem about which 'bits' of literacy we might be comparing to a verbal reasoning score. Reading single words? Spelling? Reading comprehension? Reading speed? Traditionally, the comparison has been made between IQ and the level of single-word reading and spelling.

   However, this can be misleading. An intellectually able dyslexic person who has had a reasonably good education may have compensated well enough for his difficulties to score well on simple tests of basic reading and spelling. By contrast, he may score badly on tests of higher level literacy skills, such as silent reading comprehension and structuring written work; and his reading and writing speeds may be below average. Unfortunately, there are no data available of correlations between scores on verbal reasoning and scores on higher level literacy tests of this sort.

Note on the Concept of Intelligence

It may be useful to some readers if I explain here that the IQ tests used by psychologists do more than measure intelligence in the popular sense, that is, the ability to do reasoning tasks. An IQ test looks at a much more complex and disparate set of cognitive abilities – these include not only reasoning but also perception, memory, tracking symbols, and general information-processing ability. An IQ test, therefore, could perhaps more usefully be called a 'test of cognitive abilities'.

Some assessors have decided to take flight altogether from this notion of comparing IQ (in whole or in part) and literacy. In the main, they have fled in two opposite directions. One group has opted to 'ditch' the IQ element, and to base a diagnosis of dyslexia simply on literacy skills, maintaining that if these are below average a person is dyslexic irrespective of the level of their overall intellectual ability. The dangers of this approach will be illustrated in the first case study below, so I will not elaborate on them here.

The second group of assessors who are in flight from the IQ/literacy comparison prefer to 'ditch' the literacy component, or at least to downgrade it, and to concentrate on the *cognitive profile*, that is, the profile of test results within the IQ test.

Cognitive versus Literacy Tests

The term 'cognitive' refers to all of our brain functions. It will, therefore, refer to such things as reasoning, perception, memory, *and* literacy skills. There are brain areas which 'specialize' in these three types of abilities.

In dyslexia assessment reports, however, it is the general practice to split literacy skills off from other cognitive abilities. So a typical report will have two separate sections, one called 'cognitive abilities', and the other 'literacy skills' (or sometimes 'attainment').

This second group of assessors looks for a discrepancy *not* between IQ and literacy, but within the IQ (or cognitive) profile itself. In particular, they look for higher scores on tests of verbal reasoning and perception than on tests of memory and visual tracking (the ability to follow a line of letters or numbers). An uneven cognitive profile of this sort is often referred to as a 'spiky' profile – an example of this is shown in Figure 1.1.

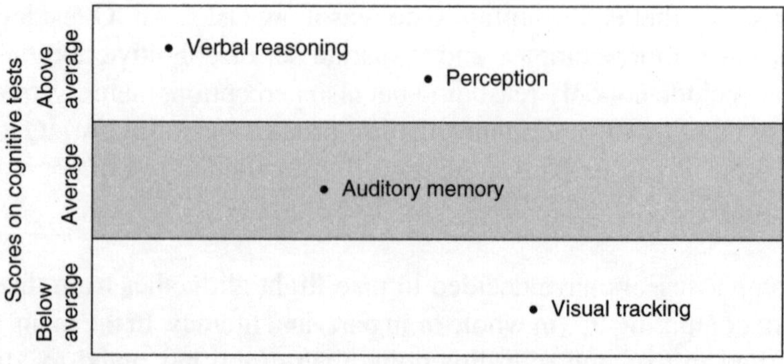

Figure 1.1 A 'spiky' dyslexia profile

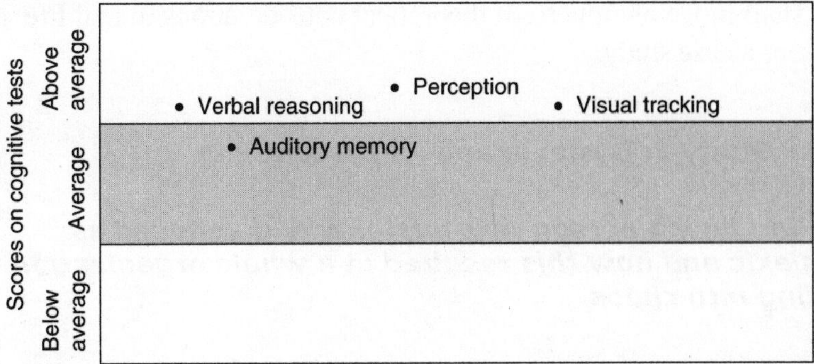

Figure 1.2 A 'flat' profile with no indications of a specific difficulty

This contrasts with a much 'flatter' profile found in people who do not have a specific learning difficulty – see Figure 1.2

Assessors who place emphasis on the cognitive profile are in effect, therefore, 'defining' dyslexia as weaknesses in short-term memory and visual tracking – two abilities which can be put together under the general heading of information-processing ability.

There is one more, very important, ability to mention in this discussion of how to identify dyslexia. This is phonology – the ability to recognize, pronounce, and sequence the sounds of a language. If you try to pronounce a non-word such as *baltiprok*, you are using your phonological skills to (i) assign a sound to each of the letters you see and (ii) sequence the sounds correctly to give a plausible pronunciation of this non-word.

Many researchers regard poor phonology as the core difficulty in dyslexia. This may be so, but from the point of view of the assessor of *adult* dyslexia, phonological difficulties may be less important than, for example, difficulties with memory or organizational skills. Poor phonology tends to manifest itself most obviously in childhood, particularly in the primary school years, when children are still trying to sound out words rather than quickly recognizing them.

By contrast, adults with dyslexia, though they may have underlying weaknesses in phonology, have often compensated well for these, and have developed good word recognition skills. However, poor phonology may still interfere with their ability to read polysyllabic words quickly and accurately, and so may affect text reading speed and comprehension.

I shall move on now from theoretical considerations to real life, and present a case study.

Case Study 1: Dyslexia and its Discontents

Telling how a person was mistakenly diagnosed as dyslexic and how this resulted in a whole organization falling into chaos

The client

I was asked to assess Adam, a 23-year-old man working as an administrative assistant in the Housing Section of a large charity. At the time I saw Adam he had been in this post for over a year. When he had originally applied for the job he had told the interview panel that he had been diagnosed as dyslexic a few years previously but had always coped well at work with the help of a part-time support worker. On his application form, he had written that he had gained six GCSEs with A to C grades.

The job

Adam was then offered his present job on the understanding that a part-time support worker would again be available. However, according to the Human Resources (HR) manager who first contacted me about Adam, it had turned out that, even with this support, he was not performing well.

Adam's job description was as follows:

- Respond to routine customer enquiries about housing availability and management.
- Maintain accurate records of rentals.
- Maintain accurate and up-to-date waiting list.
- Log complaints and contact relevant staff members.

According to the HR manager, Adam was completely unable to operate independently, and during the times when he lacked the help of his support worker, he disrupted the whole office by constantly shouting out requests for help to different colleagues. He was very inaccurate with numbers, and this obliged managers to spend a lot of time checking his work.

When the HR manager had discussed Adam's difficulties with him in a work review, Adam had said that, as his present job was more demanding than the previous one, he needed more support. In particular, he felt that he should have a full-time support worker. The HR manager had been dubious about this, and had decided to refer Adam for an up-to-date dyslexia assessment.

The assessment

The assessment was in fact delayed for some time because of a dispute between various managers in the charity about Adam's situation. It appeared that Adam had strong support from the charity's Director, who questioned the need to fund another assessment. However, Adam's line manager – a woman who had recently taken up her post and had been responsible for initially raising concerns about Adam's work – supported the HR manager's decision. Thus, it came about that Adam eventually arrived at my consulting room for an assessment.

Although not uncooperative during the assessment session, Adam clearly felt some resentment about having to be assessed again. He said he had read about dyslexia and 'it didn't go away'. He gave me a copy of his previous report. From this I saw that his previous assessment had been a sketchy screening assessment, in which only tests of single-word reading, spelling and phonology had been done.

I carried out my own assessment of Adam using the full range of cognitive and literacy tests appropriate in this case. My findings left me in no doubt that Adam's profile did not fit that of a dyslexic person: he had a 'flat' profile, and all his scores were well below average. So it was not a case of dyslexia, that is, a specific learning difficulty, but of a set of generally below-average scores. At the end of the assessment I explained to Adam that the assessment had not shown evidence of dyslexic difficulties.

There is no easy way to tell a client who fervently believes his problems are due to dyslexia that his difficulties are more general than this. Clients frequently challenge this diagnosis, and this was the case with Adam: he simply refused to accept my opinion, questioned my credentials, said that he knew he was dyslexic, that he always had been dyslexic, and that this was what his previous assessment had shown.

Meeting with managers

The following day I telephoned the HR manager and briefly outlined my findings. The manager seemed stunned to hear that Adam was not in fact dyslexic – she said that they had offered him support on the basis that he was. She asked if I would attend a meeting with her, the charity's Director, the line manager, and two other senior managers to discuss the situation.

During this meeting I explained to the managers how dyslexia is identified and repeated my opinion that Adam was not dyslexic. The Director seemed inclined to doubt my findings, or the implications of them, and opined that Adam, dyslexic or not, should be given all necessary help, even if this meant a full-time support worker. She said the charity would fund this, if necessary.

The meeting then became increasingly tense, with the line manager claiming that it was in no one's best interest for Adam to continue in the job. She asked me point blank if I felt that Adam would be able to work more independently if he was given specialist training. It is a difficult moment for an assessor when she is asked to give such an opinion, and of course one can never be absolute in one's judgement. However, I felt able to say that I thought it unlikely that Adam, even with relevant training, would ever be efficient in his present job – he was failing in every aspect of it and had no coping strategies to enable him to operate independently. The Director made some angry comments about the necessity of valuing disabled staff and left the room.

Further developments

During the next couple of days, before I had finished writing my report, I received three telephone calls:

1. The HR manager telephoned and said she had decided to 'come clean' about a few things. She said that all the managers and other staff who were in contact with Adam felt that he was incapable of doing his job and that he hindered other people from doing theirs. She said it was difficult for them to begin a dismissal process because they were worried about being accused of discrimination against a dyslexic person. She also intimated that the Director and Adam had a close social relationship outside of work, as they both

belonged to the same sports club. She said that complaints about Adam seemed to fall on deaf ears for this reason.

2. The line manager telephoned to tell me that, since word had got round the office that Adam was not dyslexic, the office atmosphere had become extremely bad. Many of Adam's colleagues had expressed angry feelings about him, and in return he had been verbally abusive to one of them. He had subsequently been sent to Coventry by the whole office. When he complained to the Director about this, he had been given a separate room to work in. You could, according to the line manager, 'cut the atmosphere with a knife'.
3. Adam telephoned to tell me that, since the results of my assessment had become generally known, he had been bullied by his colleagues, and that my assessment had put his job at risk. He said that if he lost the job he would have a nervous breakdown, and that it was 'all down to me'. I suggested that perhaps it was the difficulties in his present job that were stressing him, and that he might actually be happier in another role. He slammed the telephone down.

The final act

It seemed that this was a situation which would 'run and run', and I feared that the organization would remain in a state of tension and chaos for a long time to come. In fact, however, after two weeks there was a *deus ex machina* in the form of a sudden revelation from the HR manager. She telephoned me to say that, after my diagnosis, she had become suspicious about Adam's qualifications – supposedly six GCSEs with A to C grades. She had investigated these further and found them to be bogus. As a result of this, she had been able to successfully argue that Adam should be dismissed from his post, and Adam had apparently made no further objection.

I am not sure whether this can be called a happy ending, but it was at least an ending.

Discussion

This case well illustrates how an inadequate diagnostic assessment, a lack of knowledge in the workplace about dyslexia, and the complexities of office politics can all combine to produce a messy and unsatisfactory situation for all concerned. A case like this also puts the assessor under great pressure, as she is in the invidious position of having to keep pointing out that a person is probably unable to do a job. There can be pressure on the assessor from the employee concerned (as in the above case) who may complain that the assessor is threatening his job and ruining his life. There can also be pressure (though not in this case) from managers to minimize recommendations, because they are unwilling to give more rope to an employee they believe to be drowning not waving.

To pick one's way through these various pressures and agendas, one needs to keep a cool head and a steady nerve. Most dyslexia professionals are sympathetic to their clients' efforts to keep their jobs and feel reluctant to harm a person's chances of getting on in life. They could feel some temptation just to sign people off as dyslexic and hope for the best. However, it is not helpful for the consultant to slip into the role of sympathizer and be overgenerous with her diagnosis. Too often this simply raises expectations in both client and employer which are unlikely to be fulfilled.

There will always be cases where an assessor has to take a decision which is hard both for herself and for her client. But there would really be no need for assessments at all if everyone who had literacy and work difficulties were signed off as dyslexic because no one had the heart or the courage to decide otherwise.

There is also the question of cost. If a person's abilities are generally at a low level, then it is by no means certain that standard dyslexia support will make them competent to do the job. How much more support could be offered before the cost of it became 'unreasonable'? Would the provision of a full-time support worker be an adjustment too far?

Support workers are often found in roles where they are supporting people with physical disabilities – for example, people who are blind. In such cases, it is not usually difficult to distinguish where an intellectual grasp of the requirements of a job ends and a physical disability, like seeing a page of print, begins. In the case of dyslexia, however, there is – as ever – a blurred boundary. If a support worker simply proofreads e-mails, reports, and so on for a dyslexic employee, that might well seem within reasonable bounds; but if a support worker takes on the responsibility for taking notes at interviews and meetings, summarizing the notes, deciding which are the salient points, and then drafting a report on the basis of the summary, is this reasonable?

It can happen in some cases that a support worker has insensibly rather than deliberately begun to do almost everything for the person they are supporting, as they find that it is just quicker to do things themselves rather than keep correcting what someone has done badly. And there have also been cases where perhaps a dyslexic employee could, with support, have improved his skills had he been motivated to do so, but actually he found life easier if he continued in his inefficient ways, getting most of his work done by a support worker.

Note on the Application of the Disability Discrimination Act

There is sometimes confusion about whether the protection of the Disability Discrimination Act (DDA) extends to employees whose poor literacy skills are not due to a specific learning difficulty like dyslexia but rather to generally low abilities. In fact the DDA applies equally to both. The reason for the confusion seems to be that in the Guidance to the DDA, dyslexia is given as a specific example of a learning difficulty which would attract disability funding.

However, in the Guidance, dyslexia is given only as *one* example of a more general difficulty which, in the precise phrase used in the DDA, is: 'difficulty with memory, and the ability to concentrate, learn or understand'. Thus, in the above case study, the fact that Adam was not dyslexic did not in itself preclude him from being covered by the DDA, and so he would have been entitled to reasonable adjustments as long as he remained in his job. The point in question is not whether the DDA applies, but what is reasonable in a particular case.

Caveat Assessor: Some Reasons Why Assessments Can Go Wrong

Reliance on literacy tests alone

In the first case study, we saw how an inadequate assessment, relying solely on literacy and phonological skills, produced a false positive result, that is, a client was said to be dyslexic when in fact he was not.

Inadequate literacy testing

In a second case study, presented below, we shall see how an inadequate assessment, using too limited a set of literacy tests, produced a false negative result, that is, a client was found to be not dyslexic, when in fact he (probably) was.

The assessor-in-a-hurry syndrome

Sometimes an assessor fails to allow sufficient time for a client to formulate his answers to the three tests in an IQ battery which give an indication of a person's intellectual potential: verbal reasoning, vocabulary, and general knowledge (collectively known as 'verbal comprehension' tests). Some dyslexic people have word-finding difficulty and generally take a long time to formulate their thoughts when speaking. They may, therefore, give up too quickly on these three tests, perhaps through anxiety or embarrassment that they are taking too long to answer.

However, if the assessor stresses that there is no time limit, and encourages the client to persevere in brainstorming and throwing out ideas, the latter can often eventually work his way round to a perfectly good answer. If the assessor moves on too quickly, however, the client would get a misleadingly low score on these three verbal comprehension tests, and then the result could be a flat, rather than a spiky profile.

If such a client has the good fortune to be re-assessed at a later date by a more leisurely assessor, his score on these tests could increase by several points, perhaps even moving up from below average to above average, thereby producing a spiky profile.

The only-seeing-dyslexia syndrome

If an assessor is too focused on looking for dyslexia and does not ask the right questions in the history taking, she may fail to pick up on dyspraxic difficulties and/or attention deficit disorder.

Failing to take account of visual stress

Clients may be unaware that they suffer from visual stress and be ignorant of the advantages of using coloured overlays. If such a client is allowed to choose a helpful overlay in the session, before doing the reading tests, his reading speed can increase by 25% or more (and in some cases by over 100%). This could turn a below-average reading score into an average one.

Having the wrong expectation of a test

The *Analogies* test in the WRIT (Wide Range Intelligence Test) is sometimes regarded as being the equivalent of *Similarities*, the verbal reasoning test in the WAIS (Wechsler Adult Intelligence Scale). However, *Analogies* is much the more complex and difficult test of the two, as, unlike *Similarities*, it requires a wide general knowledge and a sophisticated level of vocabulary. It is possible, therefore, that a person who has a high score on *Similarities* may achieve just an average score on *Analogies*. In a dyslexia assessment, this means that a key characteristic of a spiky dyslexia profile (high verbal reasoning vs. poor auditory memory) may not be evident; in consequence, dyslexic individuals may be told that (a) they are not dyslexic and (b) they are less intellectually able than is in fact the case.

Case Study 2: Not Dyslexic Enough?

Telling how an able person nearly lost his job when an assessment failed to identify his difficulties

Background

Clive, an intellectually able man of 33, worked as a parliamentary researcher. He was finding it increasingly difficult to get through the huge amount of reading he had to do, and he also had difficulty with note-taking, making summaries of documents, and writing reports *to a tight deadline*. He felt that he would be able to manage all these activities if he had more time, but he was constantly falling behind with his work. He often took work home in the evenings and at weekends, and was becoming increasingly stressed and exhausted. He had discussed this with his line manager and had been sent for a dyslexia assessment. The tests results showed a flat profile, with all cognitive, literacy, and phonological tests at a very high level. There seemed to be no specific area of difficulty.

At a later date, Clive was referred to me for a Workplace Needs assessment. It had been accepted by everyone that he was not dyslexic, but his department was keen to find some way of helping him with his work. If he were not able to improve his efficiency, it was likely that he would be deployed to another role, which would essentially be a demotion.

Assessment

In his original diagnostic assessment, Clive had been asked to do tests of phonology and of single-word reading and spelling. He had also been given a simple comprehension task: a sentence completion exercise. I now supplemented these with some tests of high-level literacy skills: I asked Clive to do a timed silent reading comprehension test (using a complex text), and I also checked his text reading and writing speeds. Finally, I did some informal tests to get an idea of his ability to take notes and to précis material.

On the formal tests, as shown in Figure 1.3, Clive proved to be inefficient at reading comprehension, and, though he scored well on a speed test of single-word reading, his *text* reading and writing speeds were slow. The informal tests also showed that he did not have good strategies for notetaking or for summarizing complex text.

My opinion

In my report, I gave it as my opinion that Clive did have high-level dyslexic difficulties, and that, with appropriate training, he would be able to improve his skills in the areas in which he was weak. However, it must be admitted that the criteria for my diagnosis were somewhat

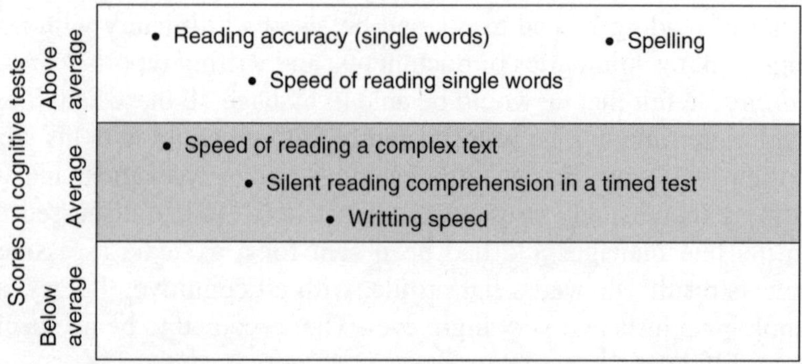

Figure 1.3 Profile of Clive's literacy skills

shaky in that, as far as I know, there are no data on correlations between scores on verbal reasoning tests and scores on the tests of higher level literacy skills that I used. From the previous assessment, I knew that Clive's phonological skills were good, and so in this case I fell back on a common sense 'rule-of-thumb' attitude to diagnosis, noting that the scores on higher level literacy skills seemed to be unexpectedly low given Clive's very high intellectual abilities.

Was I right?

I have come across this pattern of scores often enough to wish I had a name for it. The basic problem seems to be simply slowness in processing large amounts of text (presumably the inefficient reading comprehension is due to a slow reading speed), but it tends to only become manifest in situations which make particularly heavy demands on reading skills.

Following the assessment Clive received appropriate training and was able to improve his skills to a satisfactory level. He is no longer threatened with losing his job.

Comment

A general point to note here in respect of reading comprehension tests is that such tests should reflect the actual work that a client does. If one is assessing a researcher like Clive, or, say, a barrister, there is no point in using a reading comprehension test which consists of sentence completion tasks; nor is it of use to administer a comprehension test in which the client has to read material out loud while trying to remember it. The only useful test of comprehension for anybody in academic or professional life is a silent reading comprehension test, preferably timed. (The Advanced Reading Comprehension Test, developed at Hull University Psychology Department, would be a good choice.)

Case Study 3: To Be or Not To Be ... Dyslexic?

Telling how two psychologists disagreed over a diagnosis

The case in dispute

Clare, a childcare worker, wished to study for a professional qualification at her local university. She entered the university through an

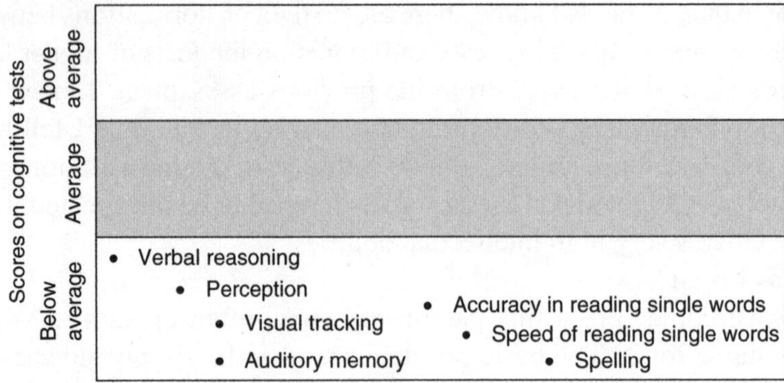

Figure 1.4 A 'spiky' dyslexia profile within a set of below-average scores

Access course, but, once she was on the course, it became obvious that she had a number of study difficulties. She was advised to have a dyslexia assessment and to apply for the Disabled Students' Allowance (DSA) to receive funding for her support needs.

Clare was assessed by a psychologist attached to the university and the test profile which emerged is shown in Figure 1.4.

Earlier (page 10) I explained that researchers associate dyslexia with a spiky cognitive profile, and Clare's test results certainly showed this. Her literacy skills were also very poor, and well below her reasoning ability. Technically, therefore, she was dyslexic. At the same time, however, all her scores, even her highest ones, were below average, and many of her scores were at the bottom of the range.

The college psychologist gave it as her opinion that Clare was dyslexic and was therefore entitled to receive the DSA. When the report was sent to the LEA (the then provider of the funds for the DSA) it was reviewed by the LEA Consultant Psychologist who rejected the dyslexia diagnosis on the grounds that Clare was basically of below-average abilities, and therefore would be unlikely to finish a university course.

Which psychologist was right?

Comment

There are a number of practical considerations that may influence a decision taken in a case like this. The first is the proper use of disability funding. Is it correct, in a borderline case, to stress the dyslexia profile, and so make the person eligible for DSA funding worth several thousand pounds? Or should one stress the below-average abilities element, and decide that the funding would most likely be wasted, because the student would probably drop out of the course? (In the case above, the student was awarded the DSA after an appeal, but did drop out of the course after two terms.)

A second related point is that there is only a certain amount of disability funding available for all the different disabilities which attract support. There is already a perception that dyslexia is taking up too high a proportion of disability budgets, and there may be a suspicion that this is partly because too many borderline or low-ability cases are being 'nodded through' as being cases of dyslexia. One result of this could be reductions in the amount of funding available to dyslexic students. Obviously, this is to the disadvantage of those dyslexic students who would, with appropriate support, be likely to finish their university course.

This is an area where there is always going to be tension. In the case study above, it may be noteworthy that the psychologist who worked for the university was in favour of the student 'being dyslexic' and so qualifying for the DSA, whereas the psychologist who worked for the LEA (the paymasters) was much more cautious in her judgement. It seems, then, that where assessors 'draw a line in the sand' may sometimes depend on the context in which they work.

So, just another of those blurred boundaries which characterize the world of dyslexia.

Conclusion

In this chapter, I have given examples of a number of ways in which dyslexia diagnoses can go astray. Sometimes it is because too limited a range of tests has been done, sometimes because the assessor has not probed deeply enough or has not conducted the session in a way which allows the client time to display their knowledge. But often it is because of the fuzzy nature of the dyslexia concept itself and the difficulty of distinguishing dyslexia from more general difficulties.

How uncomfortable and unsatisfactory it sometimes feels to be in a position where, from a welter of uncertainties, we have to conjure up a black-and-white decision about whether a client has dyslexic difficulties – because so often whether or not we put the word 'dyslexia' in a report has huge implications for a person's future life and work prospects.

INFORMATION POINT A

Dyslexic Difficulties in the Workplace

Diana Bartlett

Dyslexia affects efficiency in many workplace tasks. The list below shows a range of difficulties which are commonly reported, though, of course, no individual dyslexic person will have *all* of them. Also noted are the strengths and talents that many dyslexic people possess.

Reading

- Reading and understanding written reports.
- Reading thick files of information.
- Reading at speed or under pressure.
- Following written instructions, for example, work procedures, or protocols.
- Reading out loud, for example, at meetings, or from PowerPoint presentations.

Writing

- Expressing ideas clearly and succinctly in writing.
- Producing written work quickly.
- Writing in an appropriate style.
- Writing coherent memos, letters, and reports.
- Using correct punctuation and spelling.
- Keeping a clear logical thread and structure in a piece of writing.
- Writing down messages.
- Taking notes in meetings.
- Filling in forms or work sheets.

Dyslexia and Employment Edited by Sylvia Moody
© 2009 John Wiley & Sons, Ltd

Number Work
- Accurate copying of numbers in data entry.
- Writing down sequences of numbers, for example, account numbers.
- Understanding mathematical relations, for example, percentages.
- Recalling correct calculation formulae or procedures.
- Keeping track of numbers in complex tables.
- Avoiding over-checking.

Sequencing
- Filing documents/finding filed documents.
- Looking up entries in directories/dictionaries.
- Carrying out instructions in the correct order.
- Following work procedures.
- Prioritizing work.
- Structuring ideas in oral interactions.
- Carrying out tasks in an efficient, logical way.

Short-term Memory
- Remembering messages, instructions, and directions.
- Remembering telephone numbers.
- Recalling the content of written material.
- Following conversations, discussions, or talks.
- Formulating thoughts when speaking to others.
- Taking notes of meetings.
- Remembering people's names.
- Multi-tasking, for example, listening at the same time as taking notes.

Organizational Skills
- Poor time management.
- Inefficient work methods.
- Getting the times and places of meetings wrong.
- Missing appointments.
- Failing to prioritize.
- Failing to meet deadlines.
- Difficulty managing a varied workload.
- Difficulty carrying out complex work projects.
- Never having the right papers.
- Losing things.

- Having a chaotic workspace.
- Difficulty working under pressure.

Speaking and Listening Skills
- Interrupting in meetings, discussions, or conversations.
- Losing track of own thoughts and wandering off the point.
- Losing track of what other people are saying.
- Explaining things simply and clearly.
- Appearing abrupt or rude.

Hand–eye Coordination
- Slow and untidy handwriting.
- Poor presentation of written work or figures.
- Inaccurate keying on word processor, calculator, or telephone.
- General clumsiness or slowness.
- Difficulty with practical tasks, such as laboratory work.

Visuo-spatial Skills
- Confusing left and right.
- Having poor sense of direction.
- Getting lost in strange surroundings.
- Losing bearings in familiar places.
- Digesting information presented in visual form, for example, graphs, charts, tables of figures.
- Reading maps.

Concentration and Attention
- Focussing concentration for long periods.
- Focussing concentration when being given oral instructions.
- Maintaining concentration in conversations, meetings, or discussions.
- Susceptibility to distraction by background noise or activity.
- Losing place in a task.

Emotions
- Confusion and bewilderment.
- Embarrassment, shame, and guilt.
- Lack of confidence, low self-esteem, self-doubt.
- Lack of assertiveness.

- Defensiveness and evasion.
- Frustration and anger.
- Anxiety, stress, fear, and panic.
- Despondency, depression, and despair.

Positive Aspects

- Conscientiousness and determination.
- Holistic ways of dealing with tasks.
- Lateral thinking.
- Creativity and innovation.
- Awareness of links and associations which escape linear thinkers.
- Good powers of visualization.
- Good spatial and practical skills.
- Untaught intuitive understanding of how systems work.
- Good problem-solving skills.

CHAPTER 2

A Human Resources Manager Speaks

Brian Hagan

This chapter is a transcript of an interview with Brian Hagan, previously a Human Resources manager and now a workplace dyslexia consultant. The interview is conducted by Sylvia Moody, the editor of this book. (Throughout the interview masculine pronouns are used to refer to the HR manager, feminine pronouns to the employee.)

SM: Brian Hagan – in our interview today I am hoping to tap your expertise in both dyslexia and HR management, and in particular to ask you about how HR managers view dyslexia. To begin with, however, perhaps I could invite you to say a little about your background?

BH: Certainly – I worked for 20 years in HR consultancy and management, eventually rising to be Head of Staffing with responsibility for a multi-disciplinary team of 1600 people. At first I was involved in recruitment and selection, and later I assumed responsibility for policy development and implementation.

SM: So you have a good general overview of the HR system. In what particular settings did you work?

BH: A variety of Central Government Departments and free-standing business units within Local Government, including the Department of Employment and Camden Council.

SM: How did your move into the dyslexia world come about?

BH: Through supporting a friend who was dyslexic – I knew him to be a hard working and conscientious person, yet he was facing

Dyslexia and Employment Edited by Sylvia Moody
© 2009 John Wiley & Sons, Ltd

dismissal. I used my HR expertise to bring in dyslexia experts, and our joint efforts resulted in him being offered significant compensation for unfair dismissal.

SM: So this whetted your appetite for learning more about dyslexia?

BH: Yes, and I did a training course – at University College London – to learn how to teach adults with dyslexia, and following that I began doing dyslexia consultancy, working with both public and private sector organizations. That's where I currently am – doing that and also offering a career advice service to dyslexic people.

SM: What motivated you most to pursue this career?

BH: I think an increasing appreciation that, while dyslexia tutors knew a lot about dyslexia, and while HR professionals knew all about HR policies and practices, neither of these two groups knew much about the world of the other – I wanted to bridge the gap between them, show how each could help the other in supporting dyslexic employees.

SM: It is true that many dyslexia experts are either clinical or educational psychologists, and so, unlike occupational psychologists, they are not familiar with the workplace. What effect does this have in practice?

BH: Well, I have read quite a few dyslexia reports by psychologists which were totally unhelpful. When I was an HR manager, I would not have had much time for them.

SM: What was wrong with them?

BH: Well, for one thing they were too long – often 25 or more pages. If 10% of my staff are dyslexic, I am not going to have time to read that volume of paperwork. Also, there's too much jargon in the reports – a busy manager needs a brief operational summary of the issues, not detailed technical analyses. And, most important of all, there is no real appreciation of the realities of the way things are done in the workplace, and even, dare I say, a certain naïveté about how business in general works.

SM: The recommendations made – would they be useful?

BH: Some might. Some were hopelessly out of touch with modern business – for example, one report that came to me recommended that a social worker should have a full-time support worker shadowing her and making notes for her – this is just impractical – and unfortunately when recommendations like this are made, a report can lose all credibility.

SM: Some people do have a designated support worker though, don't they? Would it be very unusual for this amount of support to be given?

BH: I would say, yes, it would be unusual. I'm just wondering – who would pay? And I think operationally this would be quite difficult as well.

SM: What problems would you anticipate?

BH: Well, in the example I gave above – would the support worker attend interviews with the social worker, or does the social worker go out and interview somebody and then come back and brief the support worker? There are big communication problems here.

SM: Perhaps also professional issues too – I mean, would it be right for an unqualified person to be responsible for taking notes at an interview with a client? They might miss something vital.

BH: Yes, absolutely – I'm really struggling to see how this could work.

SM: We've talked about how dyslexia professionals may be ignorant of a workplace culture. Can we turn to the reverse now – managers being ignorant about dyslexia?

BH: Yes . . . and in fact there a quite a few managers who don't even believe dyslexia exists.

SM: Why is that?

BH: Well, firstly, they see it as a potential con – either people looking for special treatment, or making an excuse for poor performance. And, secondly, some managers perceive dyslexia as simply a problem with literacy, and when someone uses dyslexia to explain organizational or time management difficulties, the managers think this is nonsense.

SM: At the present time do you think there is any increase in awareness in the HR world of dyslexic difficulties and their effect on workplace efficiency?

BH: There is more awareness now than when I was working in HR, and I think this is because of organizations like the British Dyslexia Organization, and a variety of well-received books and other publications about dyslexia in the workplace.

SM: Do you think that the Disability Discrimination Act in particular has been a factor in focussing HR minds on the subject?

BH: Yes, particularly in those organizations where there is an in-house HR department – then the HR professionals will remain abreast of employment legislation and ensure that the implications of this are known throughout the organization. In smaller organizations, though, the HR may be outsourced or not present at all, and there may be little awareness of dyslexia within the organization.

SM: Would HR managers be aware that as much as 10% of their workforce could be dyslexic?

BH: Probably not – dyslexia wouldn't have a particularly high profile – it is likely to represent only one strand of what the HR managers do – one responsibility out of maybe twenty.

SM: Do you remember, in your own career in HR, if you actually dismissed somebody who in retrospect you think could have been failing in her job because of unrecognized dyslexic difficulties?

BH: No, but I do recall a case where I had complaints from one manager about the performance of a staff member who subsequently turned out to be dyslexic. But as we followed the disciplinary process through, it became clear that what we had seen as performance problems were actually caused by dyslexia.

SM: So did you put support in place and keep this person in the job?

BH: Yes, and that experience informs my work now of course. I frequently come across cases where I am called in as a dyslexia consultant, and the organization is already some way down its disciplinary process with an employee. This is where a knowledge of HR and dyslexia combine well together to help organizations to avoid disciplining an employee for what are in fact the consequences of a disability.

SM: And are employers usually amenable to halting a disciplinary process in these circumstances?

BH: Many firms welcome the opportunity to do this, but equally many managers do not welcome it because they have invested a lot of time and credibility in this being a disciplinary matter.

SM: So they would lose face if they were shown to be wrong?

BH: Yes, and another problem is that, before the matter gets to the HR person's desk, it will have gone through a number of stages at operational level, where, unfortunately, positions may have hardened. Particularly in a small organization which outsources its HR, you will have managers who are not trained in personnel management just unreflectively implementing disciplinary procedures from handbooks.

SM: It wouldn't occur to them that it might be a disability rather than a disciplinary matter?

BH: No, they would just get dragged through a series of procedural steps, and drag the dyslexic employee along with them.

SM: Would the professional HR manager, then, be more likely to pick up on the fact that inefficiency could be due to a disability?

BH: If they were conscientious and kept abreast of current literature on disability, yes.

SM: Let's say a good HR manager has picked up that an employee might be dyslexic. What action would he be likely to take to investigate the situation more thoroughly? Who would he turn to for advice?

BH: In a large organization there would probably be an internal or outsourced Occupational Health department offering diagnosis and advice on all types of disability. So that would probably be the manager's first port of call.

SM: Could there be a problem with that – isn't that putting dyslexia straight into a medical context?

BH: Yes, there could be a big problem with that. Some OH personnel tend to see dyslexia as simply due to stress, or as a mental disorder. In OH literature it is usually discussed in a medicalized context. I recently saw several dyslexic clients who had been referred by the OH department to their GPs, and in one case to a psychiatrist, for an assessment. Reassuringly, the GPs concerned and the psychiatrist all identified the problems as dyslexia and re-referred their clients to qualified dyslexia professionals – but at what psychological cost to the employee?

SM: To me an obvious thought would be that they might refer the employee to an occupational psychologist – because such psychologists are often already in the workplace advising on general organization and time management.

BH: Well, I can honestly say that in over 20 years in HR and management I have had little input from occupational psychologists. In the main they seem to be located in head office writing policy papers about what the organization might do rather than dealing with individual employees with a disability. In any case, very few occupational psychologists, in my experience, have specialist knowledge of dyslexia.

SM: Turning to another point: why is it, do you think, that so many dyslexic people seem to be in jobs which they can't manage? Does this suggest that there is something wrong with the recruitment process?

BH: Well – most recruiters will claim that their recruitment methods are designed to get the best person for the job. Some organizations do succeed in this – they do a careful job analysis to define what the job requires and set out related competencies – but some organizations don't observe best practice. Also the most common tool used to make final selection decisions is still the interview, and of course many dyslexics are able to give a good account of themselves at interview.

SM: So in that case, would you advise a dyslexic client of yours, who you thought would interview well, not to mention her dyslexia on an application form?

BH: I don't advise people either way – I just set out the different options and their implications. Not mentioning your dyslexia might get you the job but it won't necessarily help you keep the job. People getting into jobs without declaring their dyslexia leads to many of the problems that I see six months down the line.

SM: I suppose there could be a perception amongst employers that a dyslexic person is never going to be as efficient as a non-dyslexic person, even if adjustments are made – dyslexic difficulties are so broad, unlike, say, blindness, which affects just one specific ability.

BH: Yes, but it shouldn't be generalized efficiency that is being assessed during a recruitment and selection process – more the knowledge, skills, and experience required for operating efficiently in a specific job.

SM: Is there any legal requirement for a person to disclose that they are dyslexic when applying for a job?

BH: No, there isn't a legal requirement, but the dyslexic applicant may be losing out by not presenting a full picture of her background. Many employers will offer reasonable adjustments as early as the application stage – ideally their recruitment advertisement should make it clear that the organization supports candidates with disabilities.

SM: Can you give an example of something the employer could do to make the application stage easier for a dyslexic person?

BH: Yes – the employer could send the application form by email, and then the applicant could fill it in on the computer. This would allow her to enlarge the font and to use the spellchecker – and it would make it easy for her to do several drafts of the responses.

SM: So far we have talked mainly about the danger of an employee being disciplined or dismissed for inefficiency, but does it not also happen that a dyslexic employee finds a job so stressful that she herself wants to leave it. How would an employer be likely to react to this?

BH: This raises the whole question of staff retention and motivation. Too often I am called in to 'fix' problems with dyslexic employees at too late a stage. How much better if the employer had sought advice earlier on how they could be proactive in putting procedures in place to keep dyslexic employees on board. By the time I'm called in, the situation is often almost beyond repair.

SM: How would you attempt to repair a situation like this?

BH: I would try to get a good understanding of where the dyslexic employee 'is' from the emotional point of view. Very likely she will be angry, stressed or fearful – probably all three. Very often she will have been working flat out to the best of her ability to get through her work, only to receive criticism and hostility in return.

SM: So I suppose at that point you would need to see where the manager 'is' as well?

BH: Yes, I would try to turn the manager's attention away from his irritation with the employee and ask him to try to look at it from the employee's point of view – to think how he himself would feel if he were failing in a job despite his best efforts to perform it well. Very often managers have not really had an experience of failure, and they can't interpret or identify with the negative emotions and attitudes that can go with it. It's no good just someone like me coming in with advice about a load of reasonable adjustments and not tackling the feelings of hostility that have probably built up on both sides.

SM: So a general point here is that it would be much better – and perhaps less costly – for the employer if the situation had been properly thought out and dealt with at an earlier stage?

BH: Yes – I remember being called into a large market research company – they wanted to dismiss a dyslexic employee and asked me to review the paperwork. This revealed a hugely expensive process – memos about the employee's inefficiency, meetings between highly paid managers and solicitors discussing what would have probably been fruitless and discriminatory disciplinary processes. Not to mention the havoc that this all caused to team motivation. And all this long futile process could have been nipped in the bud if they had received proper advice at the beginning about reasonable adjustments.

SM: And supposing that a dyslexic employee does stay in post despite the difficulties, it will no doubt still be important to consider reasonable adjustments throughout her career – for instance in staff training and development processes?

BH: The first thing is to have a well-considered induction process. If a dyslexic employee doesn't grasp the basic skills induction provides, further training is likely to be wasted. I recently worked with a dyslexic man, a trainee manager who started an intense induction programme that required him to read and assimilate huge volumes of case material, and then be assessed on it the following day. The fact that no reasonable adjustments were in place meant that he performed poorly on these classroom exercises, and lost confidence in himself – and also credibility with his colleagues. He never recovered from this early experience and resigned halfway through his training.

SM: If the dyslexic employee survives the induction, they could still face other problems with training further down the line?

BH: Yes – training is frequently seen as the solution to poor performance. For example, a common managerial response to a dyslexic employee's poor report writing is: send them on a report-writing course. And the employee will usually come back having learnt virtually nothing – disastrous for all concerned!

SM: Presumably because the trainer has been unaware of how dyslexic people learn?

BH: Yes – and secondly because a dyslexic employee on a standard training course usually can't take effective notes, or recall the training without them. Then their subsequent 'failure' to show they have benefited from the training is likely to make managers think they are incompetent and unmotivated.

SM: So the question of dyslexia awareness comes up again and again?

BH: Yes, I feel it's very important that good practice in regard to dyslexia is embedded in HR policies and processes at every level: recruitment, training, appraisal. In fact it is just here – in the development of such policies – where dyslexia and HR should meet.

SM: Let's take up the issue of appraisal – work reviews, target setting, and so on. I suppose that this is another long-term 'hazard' for dyslexic employees?

BH: There are a number of issues here. One thing is that managers need to be imaginative in developing flexible targets for dyslexic employees – giving them the opportunity to show their strengths and expertise. Also nothing that's not essential in a job should be made a performance objective.

SM: Are there not some jobs where it might be difficult to make the targets flexible? I'm thinking, for instance, of call centre employees who have to handle so many calls in so many seconds. How flexible could a manager be in a situation like this?

BH: There could be some flexibility – the employee could be allowed slightly longer than her colleagues to deal with calls, or perhaps given longer rest breaks. I would concede, though, that some jobs that require quick reaction times are always going to be difficult for a dyslexic person.

SM: Let's take the case, then, where a dyslexic person, even perhaps with some appropriate support, is found not to be up to the job. Would re-deployment be an alternative to dismissal in such cases?

BH: Perhaps in some cases re-deployment could be seen as a reasonable adjustment. I have recommended it on a number of occasions but rarely seen it happen.

SM: Why is that?

BH: Because in my experience there is a traditional suspicion amongst HR managers of re-deployees – a feeling that 'if they are any good, why are they being transferred?' I think that re-deployment seems easier in theory than in practice. I suppose it might often be a refuge for the assessor who is casting around for some sort of positive outcome for the employee.

SM: But could there not really be a fresh start, once it was realized that an employee had been hampered by dyslexia? Maybe a career development interview, a better appreciation of the employee's strengths, and seeing whether there wasn't a position somewhere in the organization where her competences could be used?

BH: That's the sort of idea that everybody likes, but often an organization can't make it happen. That's because HR policies often require transfers to be made through a formal and demanding re-deployment process. And, of course, if your organization is small, there is often nowhere to re-deploy anyone to!

SM: Throughout our interview we seem to have been talking about dyslexic employees as doing nothing but having difficulties and posing problems – yet dyslexic people, like everyone else, have a number of strengths, even special talents. Are HR managers, in your opinion, too focussed on the difficulties to see, or utilize, the strengths of a dyslexic employee?

BH: I'm afraid that is often the case: dyslexia is usually seen at best as something to be fixed. A few best-practice companies have embedded policies which are designed to identify and utilize the strengths of their dyslexic employees, but there is still a lot of awareness work needed before this becomes standard practice. Most of the dyslexic employees I encounter in my practice are hard working, determined, and frequently have excellent IT, interpersonal, and lateral thinking skills – it would be nice if they were given more credit for them!

SM: Well, we have covered a lot of ground in this interview. We have followed a dyslexic employee through all the stages of her professional development and considered both good and bad outcomes. Are there any remaining issues you want to flag up for further thought or discussion?

BH: I would just like to emphasize again the importance of embedding good practice in policy and process at every stage of the employment cycle. Unless there is ownership of these policies at the delivery end of HR and operational practice, then nothing happens. It's not enough just to write policy – you have to integrate it seamlessly into all aspects of the organization's management.

SM: Well – I think that's a good place to end our discussion. I would like to thank you very much for giving us dyslexia professionals such a good insight into the world of the HR manager.

INFORMATION POINT B

Reasonable Adjustments

Brian Hagan

What are Reasonable Adjustments and Who is Entitled to Them?

The Disability Discrimination Act 1995 (DDA) states that employers have a duty to make reasonable adjustments to ensure that disabled employees are not put at a substantial disadvantage by employment arrangements or any physical feature of the workplace. Dyslexia will usually be considered a disability for the purposes of the DDA.

Under the Act, it is unlawful for employers to discriminate against existing and potential employees, for a reason related to their disability, in all aspects of their employment.

What is Reasonable?

Clearly the requirements for reasonable adjustments will differ from case to case. In deciding what is reasonable, managers – and dyslexia consultants – will need to consider

- the size of the organization;
- the nature of the job;
- the individual's needs.

Dyslexia and Employment Edited by Sylvia Moody
© 2009 John Wiley & Sons, Ltd

And whether the adjustments

- are practical;
- are excessively expensive – bearing in mind the size of the organization, the nature of its business, and its resources;
- will significantly reduce the disadvantage faced by the dyslexic employee;
- could cause serious disruption to other colleagues.

Ways in which an Organization can Support Dyslexic Employees

Dyslexia-friendly policies and practices need to be embedded in every aspect of an organization's policies. HR personnel and managers at all levels need to be given dyslexia awareness training so that they can effectively support dyslexic employees at all stages of their employment – in particular

- recruitment and selection;
- performance and appraisal;
- training and development.

Recruitment and selection

Employers should not use recruitment and selection methods which treat dyslexic candidates less favourably than non-dyslexic candidates. For example, it would be reasonable for an employer to

- assess only the knowledge, skills, and experience required for the effective performance of the job applied for – for example, written tests could be waived if writing were not a significant part of the job;
- assess the candidate in ways which are as close as possible to the circumstances of the job – for example, allowing applicants to use equipment or access databases that would be available to them if they were in the job;
- assess skills through observing and evaluating performance rather than asking for knowledge to be shown through written tests;

- if written tests have to be used, allow candidates extra time to complete them;
- consult with candidates about adjustments which will enable them to demonstrate their competences most effectively.

Performance and appraisal

In general, dyslexic people have problems with literacy skills, memory, organization, and communication. (See Information point A for a detailed description of dyslexic difficulties.) Performance problems caused by these difficulties often lead to a dyslexic employee being inappropriately accused of misconduct or incapacity. Managers, therefore, need to be aware of the sorts of errors which are caused by dyslexia, and to deal with these initially by offering reasonable adjustments rather than instigating inappropriate disciplinary proceedings.

As regards appraisal, managers should set realistic performance goals, and always be prepared to be flexible about setting targets. They need to offer dyslexic employees relevant training and to ensure that their working environment generally is dyslexia-friendly.

Training and development

Most dyslexic employees find that their difficulties often prevent them from benefiting from training courses. The following are recommendations for ways in which training can be made more dyslexia-friendly:

- Make available in advance the course timetable and session outlines so that potential areas of difficulty can be identified and discussed in advance with the training officers.
- Provide an overview of the course's learning objectives and session aims, so that trainees can do relevant preparation.
- Make available in advance any reading material that will be used during the training sessions.
- Provide clear notes/handouts as backup.
- Allow the trainee to record the sessions.
- Video-record demonstrations/training sessions.
- Allow the trainee to retain handouts, PowerPoint printouts, and demonstration materials after the session.

In general, trainers need to gain an understanding of the needs of dyslexic learners, and to modify course content, materials, and presentation accordingly. Wherever possible, material should be produced in PC-readable formats. It should be prepared in accordance with the British Dyslexia Association style guide (pages 19–23 in their Code of Practice for Employers), as this facilitates reading of text through the use of optimum text size, fonts, and background colours.

Where training involves work on PCs these should have screen, font, text size, and background colour modification facilities (e.g. Textic software), as these can significantly alleviate the difficulties many dyslexic employees experience with screen 'glare' and text distortions.

How Individual Managers can Help a Dyslexic Employee

A manager should identify a particular employee's needs by arranging a Workplace Needs assessment. This will

- identify the nature of the employee's difficulties;
- take account of job requirements;
- recommend appropriate reasonable adjustments.

In general, adjustments which an individual manager can usefully make are:

1. Arrange specialist workplace skills training to help the employee become more efficient in all the areas in which he/she experiences difficulty. (See Chapter 9 for detailed advice about a workplace skills programme.)
2. Arrange assistive technology support. (See Chapter 6 for detailed information about AT training and support.)
3. Take measures in the workplace which will be helpful to the employee, for example
    - assign tasks which are difficult for a dyslexic person to another employee, allowing the former to concentrate on tasks in which he/she is more proficient;
    - check back understanding of instructions in a way that engages the dyslexic employee;

- modify instructions or reference manuals to make them easier to read or follow;
- give important instructions in accessible/audiovisual formats;
- offer help with prioritizing and organizing workloads, for example, provide diagrams and flow charts rather than written schedules;
- do not expect the employee to alternate at a moment's notice between work requiring sustained concentration and work requiring rapid and variable responses.

4. Be flexible in setting targets and avoid supervisory practices which are stressful for dyslexic employees, for example, asking them to perform tasks while being directly observed.
5. Modify operational practices to deliver cost-effective help to the employee without disrupting overall work efficiency. This could include
   - providing an environment which allows dyslexic employees to focus and concentrate without interruption;
   - ensuring that customer-facing work is scheduled to avoid interrupting other work which needs sustained concentration.

CHAPTER 3

How To Do a Workplace Needs Assessment

Sylvia Moody

A Workplace Needs assessment is a complex 'operation'. The assessor not only carries out the assessment but is also responsible for organizing skills training and IT support, explaining dyslexia and related syndromes to employers, and advising on reasonable adjustments and legal obligations.

When a dyslexic employee decides to seek help and support for his difficulties, he usually turns first to his line manager. (In this chapter, masculine pronouns are used for the employee, feminine pronouns for the assessor.) The line manager then usually alerts the Human Resources manager, who in turn may hand the case on to a disability officer or occupational health advisor. One or all of these people may be in touch with the dyslexia consultant to discuss the referral and to request information and advice about assessment.

It is useful at this early stage to send the employer *written* information about dyslexic difficulties, their effects in the workplace, the scope and purpose of an assessment, and the type of help and support which is available. Workplace Needs assessments are not cheap, and employers appreciate knowing exactly what they are going to be paying for, and what they can expect from the assessment process.

If the employer decides to go ahead with the assessment, then the consultant can begin a more formal process of gathering information. This can be done through sending questionnaires both to the employee and to the relevant manager (usually the line manager). This is a

Dyslexia and Employment Edited by Sylvia Moody
© 2009 John Wiley & Sons, Ltd

particularly useful exercise because it allows the assessor to see if the employee and manager agree or disagree about what difficulties are presenting themselves. From the manager the consultant will also request a job description and a person specification for the job.

The Assessment

During the assessment, the assessor will get more detailed information from the employee about his job, and will ask the latter about his own view of his strengths and weaknesses, and also about his coping strategies. If not already completed, questionnaires on workplace and *everyday* difficulties must also be administered. (Employment tribunals base their judgements about disability on the severity of day-to-day difficulties, not job-specific workplace problems.)

The assessor will then identify the employee's needs in respect of

- workplace skills training;
- IT support;
- adjustments the employer could make in the workplace;
- concessions in psychometric tests and professional examinations.

Before Writing the Report

After the assessment, and before the completion of the assessment report, it is helpful if the assessor telephones the relevant managers and briefly summarizes her findings and recommendations. Employers greatly appreciate this preliminary discussion, and they may sometimes suggest reasonable adjustments that the assessor has not thought of. They may also raise concerns about their ability to finance some of the recommendations, and in this case the assessor must consider carefully whether all the recommendations made are in fact reasonable. For instance, if there were a recommendation that extra office space be created so that a dyslexic employee could have an office of his own rather than work in a noisy area, this might be feasible for a large organization, but prohibitively expensive for, say, a small family firm.

At this stage, it may also be appropriate to give advice on sources of funding for the support programme. The employer needs to be made aware, in particular, that the government's Access to Work (AtW) scheme will often contribute to training and equipment costs. Although AtW will not fund tuition for *basic* literacy skills (the assumption being that these would have been learnt at school), they may fund help with higher level literacy skills that are specifically related to a job – for example, notetaking, reading for research purposes, report writing. An initial AtW award could be for up to 30 hours of individual training – and this can sometimes be extended if a subsequent application is made. If the employer finances the training, there is more flexibility and it may then be possible for the employee to have help with basic literacy skills where this is necessary.

Writing the Report

The assessor should bear in mind that a workplace needs report will be read by a variety of people who have little or no knowledge of dyslexia. It therefore needs to be written in plain language, and to be structured in a way that allows the reader to quickly identify the sections of the report which he/she needs to focus on. For example, employers are not interested in the details of test scores; they simply need a summary of these. So these details can be put in an appendix for the benefit of the employee and his potential tutor. Another appendix could include information sheets for the employer on dyslexia and related syndromes. So a possible report structure is as follows:

1. Referral.
2. Background.
3. Job description.
4. Work performance
   (i) Information from manager(s).
   (ii) Information from employee.
5. Recommendations
   (a) Workplace skills training.
   (b) IT support/technological aids.

(c) Further assessment.
(d) Support from employer.
(e) Concessions for courses/tests.
(f) General information and help.

Appendix: Access to Work
(i) General information.
(ii) Quotations for equipment and training.

To illustrate what each of the above sections might contain, I shall use the notional case of Mrs Smith, a training officer in an organization which helps disabled people to find employment. (For convenience, I shall use the second person in this section, that is, address the assessor directly.)

1. Referral

In this section, you need to state what position the employee holds, who has made the referral, and for what purpose:

> Mrs Smith is a Training Manager in the Access to Employment section of a large charitable organisation. She was referred for an assessment by her line manager, Miss Beverley Johnson, because of concerns that she was inefficient in certain aspects of her work. Mrs Smith herself had suggested that this might be because she had dyslexic difficulties.

2. Background

In this section, you give an educational and occupational history, and also mention any previous assessments that have been done.

Note: It may be that an employee has previously had a diagnostic assessment that is inadequate to inform your judgement about workplace needs. For example, the assessment may only have looked at single-word reading and spelling, and not at higher level literacy skills such as reading comprehension, notetaking, and structuring written work. In this case, you are advised to carry out, or arrange, a supplementary diagnostic assessment.

3. Job description

Here you need to describe Mrs Smith's job in detail:

> Mrs Smith is responsible for employing and coaching other agencies to deliver training and for monitoring their performance. Her duties include
>
> - providing support and supervision;
> - writing session plans and reports;
> - taking Minutes;
> - contributing to meetings;
> - dealing with all relevant paperwork.

4. Work performance

In this section, you need to give, *separately*, information and opinions you have received from the employer; and information and opinions you have received from the employee. For example:

(i) Information from Mrs Smith's line manager, Miss Beverley Johnson:

> Miss Johnson reported that, although Mrs Smith was hard-working and well-motivated, she was generally ill-organised and extremely slow in carrying out her work. She had a particular difficulty with written work, which was often both inaccurate and inadequate. She found Minute-taking difficult and did not always communicate effectively in meetings.

(ii) Information from Mrs Smith:

In setting out the difficulties which Mrs Smith reports, it is useful to arrange these in sections which make it clear how particular workplace inefficiencies are related to underlying dyslexic difficulties. For example:

Memory and concentration

- Following and remembering instructions.
- Remembering telephone numbers.

- Working against a background of noise.
- Remembering where things have been filed/stored.

Writing
- Inaccurate spelling.
- Inadequate content in session plans.
- Difficulty in structuring reports.
- Writing e-mails.

It is also important to report Mrs Smith's perception of her strengths and coping strategies, and her opinion on what steps her employer might take to accommodate her difficulties.

5. Recommendations

(a) Workplace skills training

In making recommendations for skills training, you need to show how each of the recommendations you make *specifically* relates to a particular workplace difficulty, and also specify the number of hours training required for dealing with that difficulty. For example:

> Mrs Smith has to do large amounts of writing in her job, very often to a tight deadline. She finds it difficult to write in a logical manner and makes mistakes in spelling, grammar and punctuation. She therefore needs to be taught effective mind-mapping techniques to help her structure her work. To improve her accuracy in writing e-mails, she should be reminded to compose these first in a word-processing programme so that she can use the spell-checker, and then to copy the text into the e-mail.
>
> Time needed for improving writing skills: 6 hours.

It is important to make the point that training is found to be more effective if it is spread out over a period of months; this allows time for development of competence, trial of different strategies, practice in implementing new working methods, and continuous feedback to the trainer. You could, therefore, suggest an initial programme of 30 hours on the basis of, say, a 2- or 3-hour session once a fortnight over a period of 6 months. The programme could then be extended, if thought desirable. (See Chapter 9 for more information on training programmes.)

Note: Some AtW centres may state that they do not provide funding for individual dyslexia-specific training, but only for equipment. This, however, should always be challenged; a request for up to 30 hours of training is reasonable.

(b) IT support/technological aids

Again, you need to explain how particular items of equipment will be *specifically* helpful in a particular job. For example:

> Mrs Smith is generally disorganised and finds it hard to schedule work efficiently. She continually forgets what she has to do and when she is supposed to do it. A PDA, synchronised with her PC at work, would make her far more efficient at, for example, scheduling appointments and remembering times of meetings.

It is important to emphasize that the IT training should not be delivered in a single session, but should be spread out over a number of sessions, in the same way as the skills training. This is because dyslexic people are usually unable to absorb large amounts of information given in a concentrated way in a single lengthy training session. (See Chapter 6 for more information on IT recommendations.)

(c) Further assessment

In this section, you could recommend, for example, occupational therapy (for a dyspraxic person), optometry, and so on.

(d) Support from the employer

In making recommendations for helpful measures that an employer could take, it is again useful to put these in separate sections. For example:

Flexible working practices
- Allow more time than usual for tasks to be completed.
- Allow absence from work for training.
- Modify procedures for testing/assessment.

Reducing stress and anxiety

- Give advance notice of tasks whenever possible rather than setting sudden deadlines.
- Offer guidance and support with new or difficult tasks.
- Try not to interrupt Mrs Smith in mid-task.
- Do not expect Mrs Smith to take notes or dictation at speed.

(See Information point B for more information on reasonable adjustments.)

(e) Concessions for courses/tests

Here you could recommend, for example, extra time in written tests or examinations, and accommodations which might be made on training courses.

(f) General information and help

This section would contain information about the main help organizations, such as the British Dyslexia Association, and the Developmental Adult Neuro-Diversity Association.

Appendix: Access to Work

(i) General information

It is sometimes the case that when an employer or employee has paid privately for a Workplace Needs assessment, and the employee subsequently requests funding from AtW for skills and IT training, he is automatically – and unnecessarily – sent for a second Workplace Needs assessment by the AtW centre. It is, therefore, politic to put a paragraph in the report as follows:

> If Mrs Smith applies for Access to Work funding, it is important that she state clearly on her application form that a workplace needs assessment has already been done. She should include a copy of this report with her application; and highlight the words WORKPLACE NEEDS ASSESSMENT on the front page.

Otherwise she may find that she is automatically referred for another workplace needs assessment. If she is referred for a second assessment, she should contact the case worker to point out that the workplace needs assessment is already in place. Please also note that, even if a second assessment is done, the Access funding can be used to finance the recommendations made in this report.

(ii) Quotations for equipment and training

If any individual item costs more than a certain amount, three quotations need to be given. Contact your regional AtW centre to ascertain the current ceiling for giving a single quotation.

Follow-up

A dyslexia consultant's work is never done. After the assessment has been completed, and the report delivered and discussed, then the employer usually wishes to have ongoing liaison with the consultant to monitor the training programme and get further advice, as necessary, on adjustments. It may also be the case that the employer, alerted now to the problems which dyslexic difficulties cause in the workplace, may decide to arrange some staff training on this topic, and so the consultant may be called in to give a talk or to run a training day.

General Comments

From the above it is clear that a Workplace Needs assessment is a complex, lengthy, and multi-faceted process. It is important at all stages that the consultant does not fall into the role of being an advocate for the dyslexic employee, but judiciously balances the needs of both employee and management, thereby acting more like a joint expert witness in an employment tribunal.

It is also important for the consultant, like an expert witness, to be clear about what questions she can and cannot reasonably be expected to answer. For example, if an employer asks what adjustments are reasonable, the consultant can probably give a confident opinion. If, however, the employer specifically asks: 'Will this person, with the training you recommend, be able to do this job efficiently in six months' time?', then no definite answer can be given. The effectiveness of training cannot be judged until the training programme has begun.

It may be the employee, rather than the employer, who asks an unanswerable question – for example: 'Am I being unfairly discriminated against?' The assessor can do no more than give an opinion about reasonable adjustments; the question of whether there is unfair discrimination is for a court to decide. In general, it is a good idea for an assessor to scrutinize her workplace needs reports carefully and to consider whether she has stayed within her area of expertise and whether she would be prepared to defend any statement she has made in a court of law.

But perhaps the most important thing to keep in mind is that a thorough assessment, and a carefully written report with thoughtful recommendations, can make all the difference between a person keeping or losing a job.

CHAPTER 4

Dyslexia on the Front Line

Pauline Sumner

In recent years, employers have become more aware of both the strengths and difficulties associated with dyslexia. They appreciate that many dyslexic employees can compensate well for their difficulties and make a valuable contribution in the workplace. At the same time, there may still lurk at the back of an employer's mind the question of whether a dyslexic employee may, at times of great stress or in a moment of crisis, falter in some way. This question is, of course, critical when dyslexic people are employed in 'front line' professions, such as the police or fire services, where a hesitant or incorrect response could put lives at risk.

In this chapter, after briefly considering a number of 'front line scenarios' in which dyslexia might impair efficiency, I will focus particularly on concerns about dyslexia in the nursing profession. I will discuss the issue of disclosure of difficulties, and consider managers' concerns both about the efficiency of dyslexic nurses and about the impartiality of dyslexia consultants. I will close the chapter with suggestions for reasonable adjustments which can be made in the workplace to support dyslexic nurses.

Some Front Line Scenarios

Tony is a 25-year-old man who wishes to join the fire service. He has dyslexic difficulties which he has known about since childhood, and over the years he has developed good compensatory strategies for them.

Dyslexia and Employment Edited by Sylvia Moody
© 2009 John Wiley & Sons, Ltd

He has an excellent academic record. However, he still has some problems with absorbing instructions and with directional sense (telling left from right) – problems which become worse under stress.

Tony has easily been able to carry out his fire-fighting duties in training exercises, has passed extensive risk assessments, and works well as a member of a team. But . . . the question arises: in a real-life incident would he be completely reliable? Going into a burning building, pitch black, full of smoke, would he be able to absorb and follow a rapid stream of instructions from a colleague or remember set procedures practised in training? Would he, when under stress, make directional errors? Would he react quickly enough if something unexpected happened and he had to make a quick decision about what to do? Anyone, in any profession, will probably make a mistake now and again, but would Tony be more likely than other people to make errors?

Aisha is a 30-year-old probationer constable. She has mild dyslexic difficulties and these have not so far been a hindrance in her training.

While she is accompanying a senior officer on a routine enquiry, news suddenly comes in of a warning received from a terrorist organization that explosive devices have been placed in a tube station. Aisha and her colleague race to the scene to help evacuate the area. At the tube station there is confusion and panic – people shouting and running in all directions. Aisha has to direct people to the nearest exits, while at the same time helping an elderly man up a flight of steps and trying to calm a hysterical mother who has a baby in her arms. All the while she is also trying to hear and absorb instructions that are coming through on her personal radio, directing her to take various actions.

All of this, knowing that at any moment the lights may go out and there may be an explosion. In a confused emergency situation such as this, where Aisha has to simultaneously listen to instructions, give instructions, help people, and make snap decisions, can she cope with all these tasks at the same time, and make a clear decision about her priorities? If she makes a wrong decision, people could die.

Two extreme situations, and yet many professionals as part of their everyday workplace duties are called upon to make split-second decisions upon which lives may depend.

There are cases, too, where poor literacy skills could put lives at risk. In the medical and nursing professions, the need for accurate documentation is of fundamental importance – and we shall consider this further in the following sections.

The Nursing Profession

The nursing profession provides a useful context in which to consider in detail the concerns of managers about dyslexic staff, and to explore ways in which these concerns can be addressed. Nurses are very much in the front line in providing care for patients or other service users.

Management concerns

The term 'management' is being used here with a broad reference to cover: mentors, supervisors, managers at all levels in the hierarchy of hospital and community services, and administrators in the National Health Service as well as the Nursing and Midwifery Council. Management concerns will obviously vary according to the duties of a nurse in a particular environment, whether this be an operating theatre, intensive care or medical ward, or a community setting. In general, however, it can be said that managers often express concerns about whether a nurse will be able to

- read instructions, for example, for setting up and operating equipment;
- be accurate with spelling complicated medical terms;
- write handover notes and keep accurate patient records;
- accurately carry out calculations for drug administration, fluid balance charts, body mass index, and so on;
- listen to, remember, and follow instructions;
- communicate clearly and logically, for example, when speaking at multi-disciplinary team meetings;
- have good time-keeping and organizational skills;
- react quickly in emergencies and work under pressure;
- be confident about seeking help and advice when necessary.

If a nurse is dyspraxic as well as dyslexic (see Chapter 5 for more information on dyspraxia), the manager will want to be sure that she can carry out delicate physical interventions, such as giving injections. (Throughout the article, I shall refer to nurses as 'she', as the majority of nurses are female.)

In advising managers how inefficiency in any or all of the above areas may be tackled, dyslexia consultants need to make it clear that their role is not restricted to being an *advocate* for dyslexic nurses. This could antagonize managers and make them feel that they were being 'got at' or pressured to make concessions without proper consideration of patient safety. Rather, the consultant should act more like an expert witness, giving a balanced opinion and advice which takes account of disability legislation, the needs of nurses, the concerns of managers, and the interest of patients. It is, of course, not the case that *all* dyslexic nurses will, with support and training, become competent.

Another issue which managers regularly raise is the question of disclosure: they feel annoyance if a dyslexic nurse does not disclose her difficulties at the beginning of her training; and of course disclosure is the pre-requisite for the nurse receiving appropriate help and support.

In the remainder of this chapter I shall, therefore, first look at the general issue of disclosure. I will then consider in more detail the role of the dyslexia consultant in advising management on reasonable adjustments for nurses. Finally, I will discuss ways in which managers can offer appropriate help and support to dyslexic nurses.

Disclosure

It is often the case that a pre-registered nurse has been diagnosed as dyslexic (or dyspraxic) at university, but the information about her difficulties, being deemed confidential, is not passed on to an employer without her explicit consent. It may be that such a nurse will disclose her difficulties when she applies for a nursing post, and, if successful in her application, will then be able to discuss reasonable adjustments with appropriate members of staff. Once these adjustments are in place, the nurse will probably be able to carry out her duties efficiently.

Unfortunately, however, not all applicant nurses do disclose their difficulties when applying for a job because they fear that this may damage their chances of being accepted. But, if a nurse does not disclose her difficulties at the application stage, she will find it more difficult to disclose them later, if she begins to experience problems. She may well be able to deal with routine duties competently, but if a sudden emergency occurs, or she has to deal with an unexpectedly heavy workload, then she may be prone to error. And because of her feeling that she must hide her difficulties, she may fail to seek help in situations where even a non-dyslexic and/or experienced nurse would ask for support.

Below I recount the differing experiences and fortunes of Kim, a trainee nurse, who, through lack of self-confidence, delayed disclosing her dyslexic difficulties until it was almost too late; and of Meena, a newly qualified nurse, who had never made a secret of her difficulties and felt confident that they would not hinder her in her career.

Case Study 1: A Demoralized Nurse

How a 'guilty secret' almost destroyed a career

Kim is a final-year trainee nurse who is on practice experience in a clinical placement in a large teaching hospital. Throughout her time at school she had felt frustrated by her inability to easily put her thoughts into writing. She did poorly in examinations and was generally regarded as 'not being the brightest of kids'. She had been taunted by other children for being 'thick'. The situation was not helped by criticism from her family who complained that she was not working hard enough and should try harder.

Despite her difficulties, Kim was determined to train as a nurse, and she succeeded in being accepted on a training course. However, her low self-esteem continued to make her very sensitive to criticism. For example, any adverse criticism from a lecturer about one of her essays would reduce her to tears. She tended to take criticism personally rather than seeing it as constructive.

Having almost achieved her ambition to become a nurse, but still keeping her difficulties secret, she began to feel growing doubts about whether she would in fact be able to operate efficiently as a registered nurse. Although she had good rapport with the patients and their families, and was efficient in practical duties, she was continually anxious about, and ashamed of, her difficulties with writing and spelling.

When Kim's mentor, after praising her for her excellent manner with patients, mentioned a few concerns about spelling mistakes in handover notes, Kim felt mortified. Her feelings of being 'useless' intensified and she gradually became withdrawn. Her colleagues, who had initially been helpful when she asked them for assistance, now started to avoid her and occasionally even acted in an impatient or bullying way towards her.

When her mentor tried to discuss the deteriorating situation with her, Kim responded in a curt and offhand manner. Eventually, communication between Kim and her mentor broke down completely, and as her written work failed to improve, the question eventually arose as to whether she was capable of continuing her training. At this point, depressed and desperate, Kim finally blurted out an admission of her dyslexic difficulties.

For Kim, this no doubt seemed to be a low point in her life and perhaps even the end of her career aspirations. In fact, however, it was a turning point, because, once it was realized that she had dyslexic difficulties, it was arranged that she should have an assessment. Following this I was called in both to carry out an individual training programme with Kim and to advise her managers on how best they could support her on the ward.

During my sessions with Kim, I encouraged her to speak freely with her colleagues and supervisors about difficulties she was experiencing and how these could be most effectively addressed. Although diffident about this at first, Kim eventually found this continuing process of disclosure a liberating experience – helpful both practically and emotionally. Her relationship with her colleagues improved and they became more sympathetic to her difficulties.

Comment

The disastrous situation in which Kim had found herself resulted partly from her own lack of proper understanding of her difficulties, and consequent shame about them, and partly from the lack of knowledge about dyslexia on the part of her supervisors and colleagues. The latter could see that Kim was generally an able, intelligent, and well-motivated person, and so they found her difficulties – and her unfriendly attitude – baffling.

It is easy to see how, in a situation like this, a dyslexic person could become the victim of bullying. The hostile reaction on the part of colleagues can be partly a result of their frustration at the person's mistakes and perceived unsociability, but it can also represent a signal that something is wrong, that is, there are genuine worries that the person concerned cannot be relied upon to get things right or to pull their weight in an emergency – and that this could potentially put lives at risk.

Had Kim felt confident enough to explain at an early stage both the nature of her difficulties and her specific learning needs, then effective help and support could have been provided, and much suffering avoided.

Ways of Encouraging Disclosure

Managers could publicize and implement set disclosure procedures, thus sending out a message that disclosure is officially acceptable.

Managers could also organize training workshops on dyslexia and other specific learning difficulties. Nurses who had already disclosed their dyslexia could be asked to help with the planning of these workshops, and to talk in them about their own difficulties and how they overcame them. In general, open discussion about dyslexic difficulties could be encouraged amongst staff.

For further information on disclosure, and an example of a draft Disclosure Document that can be adapted according to need, see page 73.

Case Study 2: A Confident Nurse

How self-confidence makes a difference

I shall now contrast the story of Kim with that of Meena, a dyslexic woman, who began her nursing training in her late 30s. Meena had been diagnosed as dyslexic when she was at primary school and had had specialist help for her difficulties. Over the years she had also developed good coping strategies and felt that her dyslexia had not impeded her progress at school or university. She was in general encouraged by her family to take a very positive view of herself and her abilities, and she accepted the few 'weaknesses' she had as being in the nature of things and nothing to be ashamed of.

I first came into contact with Meena when she was finishing her nursing training and had been accepted for a job at a children's hospital. I was impressed by how proactive she was in doing things to help herself through the initial weeks in her new job. Before taking up her post, she arranged to visit the ward she would be working on. This enabled her to get used to the journey and to orient herself in the hospital buildings and grounds; and she was also able to talk a little to the staff about her duties. As she had got used, during her training, to talking openly with her mentors about her difficulties and coping strategies, she felt confident now about discussing these with her new colleagues. Her mentor and the ward managers were supportive and declared an interest in finding out more about dyslexia. As a result, a training workshop was organized and I was brought in to talk about dyslexic difficulties and how they could be addressed. Meena herself asked if she could contribute to the workshop and her talk, which she assiduously practised beforehand, was well received by both nurses and managers.

Meena is continuing to take initiatives to raise dyslexia awareness at her hospital. She is now helping her department to consider additional ways in which, in line with the Disability Equality Duty, they can instigate anticipatory procedures. She has been asked to use her strong problem-solving skills to design an open framework in which staff are encouraged to discuss any concerns, not just those related to disability.

Comment

These two contrasting stories of Kim and Meena illustrate the great importance of dyslexic difficulties being openly recognized both by the person who experiences them and by their work colleagues. When the difficulties are not recognized, or kept a secret, a bad situation usually turns into a worse one. However, confident individuals who have learnt to 'live comfortably with their dyslexia' are likely to achieve a high degree of competence in their job despite their difficulties, and to elicit the best possible help and support from their colleagues.

Talking to Managers

A dyslexia consultant is accused of not giving impartial advice

In my experience managers are very willing to give help to dyslexic nurses and to learn more about dyslexic difficulties, the way these difficulties may impact on efficiency, and the best ways of tackling them. However, as noted earlier, some managers may have serious doubts about how well a dyslexic nurse would cope on a busy medical ward. This came out clearly in a meeting I was asked to attend with various members of staff during the period that I was helping Kim with her difficulties (see page 62). Present at the meeting were Kim's mentor, three managers, the placement facilitator, and a member of the university staff.

During the meeting, Kim's ward manager voiced various concerns he had about dyslexic nurses in general, giving some examples of where he felt handover notes had been grossly inadequate and had constituted a risk to patient care.

As I began to address this question, the manager broke in, addressing me in a hostile and impatient way. He said that I was painting far too rosy a picture of the ability of dyslexic nurses to improve their efficiency to a level that would pose no risk. He felt that I was not looking at the situation impartially, but that I was 'on the nurses' side'.

He was supported by a more senior manager who said that I obviously did not appreciate how much a patient could be put at risk by inefficient nursing. She said that, when I was suggesting reasonable adjustments, I should be thinking of what was reasonable for the patients and their safety, not just what was helpful to the nurse; I should also be thinking of what was reasonable to ask senior nursing staff to do. They were often too busy to give the amount of attention I suggested to junior staff – they would have to neglect their own duties to do so. Nobody in the room challenged these two speakers.

I replied by saying that I did not see my role as being an advocate for nurses, but rather I was trying to facilitate a negotiation process which would produce a correct balance between the interests of all interested parties. I pointed out that I had never made the claim that all dyslexic nurses who received extra help would, as a result of this, be able to manage a particular job. Each case needed to be judged on its merits. In doubtful cases, my advice would be that a nurse who was failing should at least be allowed a trial period during which she would receive specialist training. Then, before a final decision was made about her future, everyone could be sure that they had attempted to make reasonable adjustments as required by the Disability Discrimination Act.

Other people then spoke up to say that any trainee nurse, dyslexic or not, might pose some risk to a patient through lack of experience, and this was true in all 'caring professions'; the way round this was to be sure that supervision was adequate. Other people then pointed out that it was not possible on a ward, where emergencies might arise at any time, for supervision always to be available at the moment when it was required.

The general view at the end of the meeting was that, yes, any inexperienced employee in any profession might pose some risk, but with a dyslexic nurse that risk might be a little higher than average, and therefore supervisors had to be more vigilant.

If it turned out that a nurse could not be trusted to work independently in her role, then she would have to be considered for redeployment or dismissal – she should not be kept in her job simply because managers feared that they might be accused of being guilty of discrimination.

In the case of Kim, it was felt that she was making considerable improvements now that reasonable adjustments had been put in place. A decision was made that she should continue to have specialist tuition and support on the ward, and that her clinical placement should be extended so that she would have time to demonstrate improvement in her performance.

Comment

Reflecting later on this meeting and the issues that had been raised, I asked myself whether there was actually some truth in what the two hostile managers had said. Working with dyslexic people in various professional settings, I aim, as an adviser, to balance the needs of all parties, but perhaps I could sometimes insensibly slip into the role of advocate – seeing a dyslexic nurse who was failing as a victim of ignorant managers.

Perhaps I do not think enough about how a manager can be the victim of a dangerously incompetent dyslexic nurse, especially a nurse who has not disclosed that she is dyslexic. Do I need to take more account of the pressures which managers are under – their need to balance their obligations under the DDA with both their duty of care to patients and their need to meet efficiency targets?

Consciously at least, I tend to view myself either in the role of an expert witness giving impartial opinions, or in the role of mediator trying to negotiate solutions which balance the interests of all parties. Perhaps in future, when I am talking to managers, it would be better if I stated explicitly how I see my role – both to keep myself mindful of my 'neutral position' and to give reassurance to the managers. It is probably only natural that any professional who has the word 'dyslexia' tagged to his/her title is likely to be seen as being on the side of the dyslexic party or parties in any situation where conflict arises.

Training and support from management

On page 59, I noted the general concerns expressed by managers about ways in which dyslexic nurses might be inefficient. Now I shall return to these difficulties again, describing them in more detail and suggesting ways in which managers and colleagues could be helpful in alleviating them. It is important to be aware that dyslexic adults will present with a combination of *some* of these difficulties at varying levels, and may well have already developed good coping strategies in certain areas. It is important, therefore, that they are consulted about their particular needs when a support programme is being drawn up. (For details of a general workplace skills training programme, see Chapter 9.)

Reading. Dyslexic people may sometimes give the impression that they are reading quickly and easily, but what is often happening is that, due to visual stress or difficulty with word decoding, they are actually skim reading, and so they may miss out important words or skip whole lines in a text. A dyslexic nurse, therefore, may have difficulty in assimilating written documentation, such as patients' medical records, handover notes, or instructions about operating equipment. In particular, abbreviations and medical terms containing the same or similar affixes will be difficult to decode. Thus, the nurse may find that she needs to read and re-read such material *slowly* to gain full understanding.

Ways to help:

- Allow a longer time than usual for reading tasks.
- If possible, provide a quiet space for reading away from noise or interruption.
- Check for understanding of what has been read.
- Encourage the nurse to use coloured overlays and tracking rulers.
- Encourage administrative staff to provide/use coloured paper with text in easily readable fonts.

Spelling. Spelling is becoming less of a concern nowadays because of the widespread use of spell-checking facilities on computers.

However, while the availability of computers on wards is increasing, handwriting is still heavily relied upon. Incorrect spellings, especially in notes about medication, could have serious consequences.

Ways to help:

- Introduce into the ward, where possible, computers or hand-held spell checkers with specialist medical vocabulary.
- Encourage the use of personalized dictionaries in a pocket-size index book, where nurses can compile their own list of spellings they find difficult.
- Encourage and support the implementation of a multi-sensory spelling programme which includes difficult terminology.
- Suggest mnemonics which can be used to aid recall of common prefixes – for example, a mnemonic for *psycho* could be *p*lease *s*ay *y*ou *c*an *h*elp *o*ut.

Writing. A nurse who feels conscious of her spelling difficulties may feel anxious when writing – and so may scribble down notes in an illegible way to avoid drawing attention to possible spelling errors. The result may be that neither she nor anyone else can read back her notes. Dyspraxic nurses, in particular, are likely to have poor handwriting, even when they are not anxious or stressed. (For more information on dyspraxia see Chapter 5.)

Ways to help:

- Design and provide templates for handover notes and patient records, using colour-coded sections.
- Allow extra time for writing tasks.
- If possible, provide a quiet space for writing away from noise or interruption.
- Take time to check written work.
- Discourage the use of abbreviations.
- Offer extra support/supervized practice.

Numeracy Skills. A particular area of concern about dyslexic nurses is whether they will be able to accurately carry out calculations for drug administration, fluid balance charts, body mass index, and so on. Dyslexic nurses are themselves very conscious of their difficulties in this respect and generally take care to double- and even treble-check their calculations. The requirement for nurses to work in pairs, checking each other's work in areas such as drug administration, reduces the risk of error.

Ways to help:

- Allow extra time for calculations to enable notes to be made and information to be double-checked.
- Encourage the use of a calculator to re-check calculations.
- Arrange some sessions with a dyslexia tutor who specializes in teaching maths to nurses and other health workers.
- Use visual diagrams, flow charts, and mnemonics to aid memory of calculation procedures.
- Employ hands-on practice using actual equipment, such as syringes and measures.

Oral Skills. Dyslexic people may have some word-finding difficulties, and they may generally find it hard to communicate verbally in a succinct way. These difficulties will be compounded by anxiety if they are speaking in a formal setting, for example, in a multidisciplinary team meeting. Whereas non-dyslexic nurses might rely on written prompts when they are reporting a case, a dyslexic nurse may find that reading notes actually adds to her difficulties and makes her more anxious. Some dyslexic individuals are, by contrast, verbally fluent, but may still need assistance in keeping focussed on the topic they are speaking about.

Ways to help:

- Encourage nurses to thoroughly plan what they are going to say when reporting a case to a meeting.
- Encourage the use of presentation software or concept mapping programmes to assist in organization of ideas/points to be made.
- Advise nurses that, if they feel they have failed to make some points clearly in a meeting, they should e-mail relevant colleagues later to remedy the omissions.

Memory and Listening Skills. Dyslexic people often have poor short-term memory and so have difficulty in listening to, and absorbing, sequential information. So, if a manager speaks rapidly when giving instructions, the nurse may lose track after a couple of sentences.

There could also be a problem with taking, and passing on, telephone messages, especially when these include telephone numbers, e-mail addresses, or difficult names. And if, as is often the case, the nurse has been called away from another duty to answer the telephone, she will need not only to remember the telephone message but also to remember what she was previously doing, and what still needs to be done on that particular task.

Ways to help:

- Speak slowly and repeat things if necessary.
- Check that instructions have been understood by asking the nurse to repeat them.
- Allow plenty of time for instructions to be written down.
- Allow the use of a notebook or voice recorder to jot down/record important information.

Organization and Working under Pressure. Organization and time keeping are things which a dyslexic person tends to be either very bad at or very good at. At one end of the continuum there are those who are always in a muddle, missing appointments, forgetting where they have put things, and having a chaotic work schedule. These individuals may have difficulty getting to work on time, briefing and organizing other staff members, preparing papers for a ward round and drawing up patient care plans in a timely way. At the other end of the continuum are those who have made a particular effort to train themselves to be organized. These people have developed good routines and effective strategies to ensure that they operate in an efficient way. However, even such organized individuals may face problems if they have to take on unfamiliar tasks at short notice.

Ways to help:

- Encourage the design and use of colour-coded daily/weekly planners, daily prioritized task lists, diaries, and so on.
- Allow time in daily schedule for planning.
- Prepare in advance frameworks that can be used for as many different contingencies as possible, especially emergency situations where speed of reaction will be of the essence.

Clumsiness. Dyspraxic nurses may have practical difficulties on the ward because of clumsiness. For example, a steady hand is needed in setting up equipment and administering injections. If clumsiness is a major problem, it is not an easy matter to remedy. Some sessions with an occupational therapist may help, but perhaps a better solution would be for the nurse to consider making a career in an aspect of nursing in which good physical coordination was not so important, for example, in a learning disabilities unit.

Confidence. Nurses who have struggled through their education without their specific difficulties being recognized, and have possibly often been called 'stupid' or 'thick', may have very low levels of self-esteem and confidence and may be reluctant to discuss their difficulties or to seek help.

Ways to help:

- Work closely with dyslexic individuals, focussing on their strengths and abilities.
- Point out that they are often capable of achieving what they previously had thought was not possible.
- Encourage open discussion on the ward of specific difficulties.

Conclusion

This chapter has provided an overview of the issues around dyslexia which come up in nursing, as in other front line professions. It has highlighted the importance of dyslexic nurses disclosing their difficulties at the beginning of their training, so that colleagues and management can give appropriate help and support. Suggestions for reasonable adjustments have been made, and it has been noted that support programmes should be tailored to take account of each individual's strengths and weaknesses. Consideration has also been given to the danger that a dyslexia consultant may be perceived by management as being an advocate for dyslexic nurses rather than an impartial adviser. Finally, it has been emphasized that safety and fitness for practice proficiency standards apply to all front line professionals, whether dyslexic or non-dyslexic.

INFORMATION POINT C

Disclosure Guidelines

Pauline Sumner

An open and inclusive approach to dyslexia and other specific learning difficulties is an essential element in the operational efficiency of an organization and in the well-being of its employees. Of particular importance is the putting in place of standardized and well-publicized procedures which job applicants or employees can use to disclose their difficulties, report their strengths, and coping strategies, and explain what sort of help and support is useful to them.

In this short 'Information point' chapter, I shall look at

- why some people find it difficult to disclose their dyslexia;
- reasons why disclosure is helpful;
- ways of encouraging disclosure.

At the end of the chapter, I give a suggested format for a disclosure form.

Why Some People Find it Difficult to Disclose their Dyslexia

It is often the case that dyslexic people have for many years suffered their dyslexic difficulties in silence. They have come to feel embarrassed, even guilty, about these difficulties and may have been subject to ridicule, or even bullying, because of them. As a result, they may be fearful of discussing their difficulties openly with other people and may also feel hesitant about mentioning any strengths or abilities they

Dyslexia and Employment Edited by Sylvia Moody
© 2009 John Wiley & Sons, Ltd

may have. This not only results in personal distress for the individual concerned, but interferes with both efficiency and interaction with colleagues at work. As noted in Chapter 8 (page 135), it can be many years before a person plucks up courage to approach their line manager and suggest that they might be dyslexic.

Also, some dyslexic people will see no reason to discuss their dyslexia with their managers, as they feel that it does not impact adversely on their work. However, they may find that, if they are promoted or take on additional duties, then they will be in need of some extra support or job adjustments.

Other reasons a person may not disclose are that they

- have developed effective compensatory strategies and therefore feel there is no need for concern;
- prefer to keep personal matters confidential;
- worry that lack of understanding about dyslexia may result in discrimination against them;
- want to avoid being 'labelled'.

Reasons Why Disclosure is Helpful

Disclosure will

- enable reasonable adjustments to be made and support mechanisms to be put in place;
- establish eligibility for Access to Work funding for reasonable adjustments/support;
- alleviate the employee's anxiety about keeping dyslexia as a guilty secret;
- raise awareness and encourage a clearer understanding of dyslexia and related issues;
- encourage the opening up of communication channels between the employee, managers, and other members of staff;
- enable the individual to benefit from individual workplace skills tuition and IT training.

Disclosure may also

- reduce fear of disclosure amongst other members of staff;
- lead to the setting up of support groups for dyslexic employees.

Ways of Encouraging Disclosure

Ideally, dyslexia will be disclosed when an individual applies for a job. However, this does not always happen, for the reasons noted above, so it is important that opportunities are made available at different stages of the employment process for employees to disclose their difficulties. Below are suggestions for some simple and inexpensive ways in which employers can actively encourage disclosure.

Job advertisements

- Demonstrate an open and positive approach to equal opportunities in job advertisements.
- Provide the name and contact details of a person who can be contacted to discuss any concerns about the vacancy or place of employment.
- Offer application documentation in different formats.

Organization's web site

- An accessible and user-friendly web site will demonstrate the organization's commitment to equal opportunities.
- Employee profiles could include a dyslexic member of staff.
- Easy access should be provided to the organization's disability/equal opportunities policy.

Application and selection

- When asking about disability on an application form, allow plenty of space for the applicant to provide detailed information about their difficulties and strengths. Suggest that they may add more information in a separate letter if necessary.
- The application pack should contain
  - information about how adjustments to interview procedures and selection tests can be arranged with the applicant prior to the date of interview;

- the organization's equal opportunities policy;
- name and contact details of a person who can provide further information.

Employment

- Provide information (in accessible format) during the induction process on
  - the organization's equal opportunities/disability policy and procedures;
  - the Disability Discrimination Act, the rights of employees and duty of employers to uphold those rights;
  - procedures regarding confidentiality and the granting of consent for information about a person's dyslexia being passed on to others.
- Establish a mentor system whereby new employees are supported by an experienced member of staff who can provide advice and support on a confidential basis.
- Implement and publicize set procedures for disclosure, which demonstrate that it is officially acceptable to disclose in an open and formal manner. This documentation should be in a clear and accessible format.
- Encourage open discussion about difficulties between staff.
- Publicize the name and contact details of the Disability Officer or another named person who can give advice to dyslexic employees.
- Organize disability equality training, including awareness training in dyslexia, dyspraxia, and other specific learning difficulties. Include employees who have these difficulties in the planning of workshops, and encourage them to gives talks in the workshops about their difficulties and coping strategies.
- Offer follow-up emotional support/counselling after disclosure and the dyslexia assessment process which may follow.
- A Disclosure Document can be used to
  - encourage communication between manager and employee;
  - enable discussion of difficulties;
  - invite suggestions for reasonable adjustments.

Below is a suggested format for a Disclosure Document that can be adapted for any job.

Disclosure Document

This document is intended to encourage employees to openly discuss their dyslexic or other specific learning difficulties with their managers in order to determine what training or job adjustments may be appropriate.
Section 1. Information from the employee

Employee's Name, Position, Department, and contact details

If you are unsure about how to complete this form or wish to obtain further information about the disclosure process, please contact: (name and contact details for relevant person). All communications will be treated in strict confidence.

Describe the nature of your specific learning difficulty (e.g. dyslexia, dyspraxia, dyscalculia, ADHD, and so on)

Have you been assessed? Yes/No

If yes, please give date of assessment

(You will be required to produce evidence of your assessment.)

What are the key duties required in your position? (If possible, attach a job description.)

What difficulties do you experience in your job?

If you have previously received any support, what have you found particularly effective?

What do you feel are your strengths?

What coping strategies have you developed? (e.g. using assistive software or a voice recorder.)

Section 2. To be completed by the manager

This section of the form is to be completed by the manager following discussions between the manager and the employee and, if appropriate, a dyslexia consultant.

The examples below show how each difficulty can be listed with a note of the relevant support which has been agreed.

1. Handwriting not easy to read – concerns about writing up notes about patient/clients.

   Printed templates to be designed for each type of record needed. These to be colour coded to link with alphabetic filing system.

2. Difficulty in remembering long lists of verbal instructions.

   Allow extra time for notes to be taken and/or use of voice recorder where appropriate. Check back for understanding.

Etc.

Employee's Signature:

Date:

Manager's Signature:

Date:

CHAPTER 5

Dyspraxia: Problems and Solutions

Sarah Howard

Most employers nowadays are aware of dyslexic difficulties; some may also know the term 'dyspraxia', but few have a clear understanding of what dyspraxia is, or how it affects efficiency in the workplace. In this chapter, I shall describe the difficulties denoted by the term dyspraxia, and give examples from the workplace of how these difficulties can be managed. (In this chapter, feminine pronouns refer to the trainer, masculine pronouns to the trainee/employee.)

The core meaning of the word dyspraxia is: a difficulty with the planning and organization of movement (or, more simply, physical coordination). It comes from the Greek word *praxis*, which means 'doing' or 'acting'. So a dyspraxic person may have difficulty with, for example, hammering in a nail or walking up an escalator.

Also associated with dyspraxia are difficulties with

- spatial judgement (e.g. judging the distance of an approaching car);
- social judgement (e.g. knowing how to turn-take in conversations);
- learning, memory, and concentration;
- speaking and writing skills;
- work organization;
- sensitivity to noise, light, and movement.

Dyspraxic people often also have emotional problems, such as low self-confidence and poor tolerance of stress.

Dyslexia and Employment Edited by Sylvia Moody
© 2009 John Wiley & Sons, Ltd

It should be emphasized that these difficulties represent a *typical* dyspraxic syndrome. This does not mean that the difficulties are unique to people with dyspraxia; nor does a person need to have *all* the difficulties listed above to be considered dyspraxic. Some dyspraxic people may, for example, be physically clumsy but socially graceful. It is also useful to note that there is inevitably some overlap between the areas of difficulty: for example, bumping into doors may be due to poor physical coordination or poor spatial judgement, or a combination of both.

Dyspraxia is sometimes also referred to as 'developmental coordination disorder' and, although some researchers distinguish between the two, most people in the United Kingdom use the term dyspraxia to cover both. It is estimated that dyspraxia affects about 10% of the population, with about 2% being severely affected. There is often an overlap between dyspraxia and related conditions, such as dyslexia, attention deficit disorder, and attention deficit hyperactivity disorder. People with Asperger's Syndrome, who have difficulty with social and emotional relationships, are often also dyspraxic.

One of the reasons why dyspraxia is less well known than dyslexia in a workplace context is that it is less easily recognized in adults than in children. Many people who were 'clumsy' as children will, by the time they reach adulthood, have learnt to take special care when engaging in any physical activity. In fact, with practice, most dyspraxic adults become able to competently perform almost any physical movement – indeed some can develop great expertise in certain areas: they may excel at sport, for example, or in a job, such as joinery, that demands considerable manual dexterity. However, although many dyspraxic adults will not show obvious signs of being physically clumsy, they may retain many of the less visible difficulties, such as poor memory or poor organizational skills.

In the following pages, I shall describe in more detail the main areas of dyspraxic difficulty and give examples of ways in which these difficulties can be managed in the workplace.

Physical Coordination

Physical coordination can be divided into two areas: gross motor coordination and fine motor coordination.

Gross motor coordination

This refers to large movements, such as walking, running, jumping, riding a bicycle.

One of my dyspraxic clients, Annie, had difficulties of this kind. As a child she had been very clumsy, and had never been able to ride a bicycle. In her 20s she had tried to learn to drive a car, but gave up after failing her driving test six times.

Annie now works as a computer technician in Milton Keynes. She lives 4 miles from work and until recently travelled to work by bus. This caused some problems, however, as the bus service became increasingly erratic, and Annie was constantly being late for work.

I suggested to Annie and her managers that another effort could be made to help her learn to ride a bicycle. Annie herself was enthusiastic about this, so I referred her to an occupational therapist (OT). The OT worked on coordination and balance using a tilt board, floor exercises, and eventually a bicycle. In addition, the OT recommended swimming and a martial arts class to help Annie continue to improve her bilateral coordination. After a month Annie had built up enough confidence to ride the bicycle to work.

Fine motor coordination

This relates to manual (and in rare cases podiatric) dexterity, that is, using the small muscles in the hand (or foot) to carry out tasks such as writing, picking up objects, turning pages, typing, using a telephone keypad, or sending texts.

Matt, a child and family worker in Cambridge, is both dyslexic and dyspraxic. His dyspraxic difficulties particularly affect his handwriting, which is large, slow, and untidy. His job requires him among other things to interview clients either in person or on the telephone, and to make notes both of what they say and of his response. In these situations he tends to scribble even more than usual, and is often able to read back only about 50% of his own writing.

At my suggestion Matt was supplied with a digital voice recorder. He was able to use this after speaking to clients on the telephone to dictate quick notes to himself, recording what the client had said, what response he had made, and what action (if any) needed to be taken.

He felt less comfortable using the recorder in face-to-face meetings with clients, as he thought the client would be worried that confidentiality was not being respected. Eventually, he solved this problem by, first, explaining to his client that he would occasionally make an oral note to himself of important points during the session; and, secondly, by holding the recorder very close to his own mouth so that it was clear that he was not recording the client's words.

Matt soon became practised in talking with the client and then stopping very briefly to dictate a few key words to himself before smoothly carrying on with the interview. Although initially he had feared that this might seem awkward, in fact it proved to be useful not just to Matt but also to his client – it gave the latter a few moments to reflect on what had been said and perhaps to re-phrase something or make an additional point.

Matt was also able to use the recorder to record meetings – and this relieved him of the burden of having to take notes during the meeting.

As Matt's typing and handwriting were both poor, I recommended that he be supplied with Dragon NaturallySpeaking (speech recognition software) and 2 hours of assistive technology training. Matt found this an excellent solution as it enabled him to send e-mails, write up his notes, and write reports much faster than before. He has now learned how to transfer his speech files from his digital recorder to his PC where they can be converted into text.

As there were some situations in which Matt had to use handwriting, I gave him a series of hand exercises to strengthen his finger muscles. In order to improve his wrist and hand stability, I recommended that he be provided with an angled board to write on, and advised him to try out a variety of pens to see which he found most comfortable. Finally, I worked on getting him to 'join up' his handwriting. After a series of five sessions he had improved both the legibility and speed of his handwriting. I also worked with Matt to help him devise a system of abbreviations that made sense to him when he was taking handwritten notes.

Spatial Judgement

Spatial judgement is the ability to see where an object is located in relation both to ourselves and to other objects or persons. It can also involve judgement of time, distance, and speed. The following example from cricket will illustrate this: if you were a fielder in a cricket match, and at a certain moment the batsman lobbed a ball into the air in your direction, you would have to judge

- where the ball was at a particular moment in time;
- how fast it was travelling;
- where it would be a few seconds later;
- whether you or another fielder in the vicinity was closer to the ball and should try to take the catch.

Everyday examples of situations where spatial judgement is required are walking through a doorway, parking a car, finding our way in a building or in the outside world, estimating how long it will take us to complete a task, and deciding if we can squeeze onto a crowded tube train. More complex tasks in working life might be analyzing and interpreting graphs, architectural drawings, x-rays, or maps. For example, a scaffolder needs to be able to interpret an engineer's map so that he can erect scaffolding in the correct way, rather than making a rough guess at its position.

There are times when poor spatial skills can have, if not tragic, at least comic results. Diane, a clerk in an architect's office, found that her poor spatial skills had unfortunate consequences when, on her first day in her new job, she was asked to take on the task of ordering lunch (in the form of sandwiches) for everyone in the office. Her manager thought that this would be a simple task and that it would enable Diane to introduce herself to the rest of the staff in an informal way.

However, the system for ordering the sandwiches involved Diane ticking the correct small box in a complex table which had the names of staff members along the top and the names of sandwich ingredients down the left-hand side. Diane found it very difficult to keep her place in this table, and so, on that day, most people in the office received a 'surprise lunch'.

Diane's manager decided that he would not ask her to undertake this task again, but the following week, when Diane was more familiar with her surroundings and more comfortable with her new colleagues, she herself asked if she could attempt the 'sandwich run' again. Admiring her pluck, the manager asked a colleague to sit with her for a few minutes and help her by highlighting different lines in the table in different colours so that Diane could easily keep her place. The colleague then accompanied Diane round the office to make sure that she had understood how the system worked and had marked the table correctly. On that day everyone in the office was relieved to receive their correct order.

Other spatial difficulties can be alleviated by the use of technology. For example, a person who has difficulty finding their way around, even in familiar surroundings, can be supplied with a satellite navigation system (sat nav). A dyspraxic person who uses this system, however, may have to be reminded not to get so absorbed in looking at the display screen that he crosses roads without looking. For people who do not have a sat nav, other ways of remembering routes are to notice landmarks as they go along or, if they have a digital voice recorder, to record the names of streets that they walk along, again noting, if possible, a landmark at the corner of a street – whether this be a coffee bar or simply a house number if they are in a residential street.

Another example of technical support would be the provision of a screen-reading ruler (a piece of software) for employees who have difficulty in reading complicated visual arrays on the computer screen. The ruler highlights and magnifies part of the screen in a horizontal band, and can 'grey out' areas which do not immediately need to be viewed.

Difficulty in judging time can result in dyspraxic people being late for appointments. They might find it difficult to estimate, for example, how long it will take them to travel on a bus or tube between two points, perhaps making erroneous judgements on the basis of a skeletal map of bus routes or tube lines. It is handy to know that many local transport authorities have a helpline which people can ring to ask exactly how long it will take to travel between two points.

Many dyspraxic people like to practise a journey, sometimes in their own time, before the day that an important meeting away from the office will take place. This means that they will be confident of arriving the following day for their meeting on time and in an unflustered state.

Social Skills

We live not only in a physical space, but also in a social 'space'. In the latter, we need to make spatial judgements both literally and metaphorically. For example, we need to decide how close we should sit to someone, and how to apportion the 'conversational space' so that both parties to the conversation do their fair share of talking and listening. We also need to judge the correct volume at which to speak and also to adopt a manner which does not appear to be either too intrusive or too distant. And, finally, we need to be aware of what signals, verbal or non-verbal, we are giving to the other person, and to 'read' the signals that we receive from them.

Probably the best way for a person to learn good social skills is to attend a social skills course or to work with an individual trainer. One exercise the trainer might use would be to ask a dyspraxic client to role-play an interview and to record this for subsequent analysis. This would allow observation and discussion of tone and volume of voice, rate of speech, signs of hesitancy, tendency to prolixity, or talking off the point. A video recording would be even better, as that would allow non-verbal signals also to be observed and discussed.

Dyspraxic people can also learn, at least to some degree, to monitor and modify their own behaviour. They could, for instance, keep one ear on themselves during a conversation to see if they are doing all the talking. If so, they need to find ways of bringing themselves to a halt and inviting the other person to talk more. They might do this in a subtle way, for example, by just looking enquiringly at the other person, or, if necessary, more candidly by saying something like: 'Oh, I'm talking all the time again – let me know what *you* think about this. . .'.

They could also be encouraged to consciously note the reactions of their interlocutor(s). Are they bright-eyed, interested, nodding agreement, engaged – or are they looking away, fidgeting, yawning, and not troubling to respond? Sometimes dyspraxic people may seem to be completely unaware of another person's presence and so come across as rude or selfish – when in fact they may simply be displaying poor social skills.

Learning, Memory, and Concentration

Difficulties with learning, memory, and concentration are common to both dyslexic and dyspraxic people. Such difficulties are due to weaknesses in short-term (auditory) memory and slowness in processing information. Processing information, which is a mechanical activity, can be contrasted with analyzing information, which is an intellectual ability – two completely different things.

Sometimes people who are slow in processing information think that they have a hearing difficulty, as they often find themselves asking people to repeat themselves. However, this is not usually because of hearing problems, but because part of the sentence has not been 'caught' or processed. Because of this limited short-term memory capacity, dyspraxic people can have the sense of being quickly overwhelmed by incoming information; they soon reach the point of not being able to take in anything more. This memory weakness in turn often leads to poor concentration. It often also causes anxiety, thereby creating a vicious circle – the more anxious a person becomes, the less well their memory functions.

In the workplace, poor short-term memory can cause a particular difficulty in absorbing and remembering instructions. An example will show how this difficulty can lead to damaging mistakes.

Meg, a part-time PA to an osteopath, was aware that she had dyspraxic difficulties and had learnt to be very careful in her work. She did everything slowly but meticulously and was greatly valued by her employer. However, she did not always absorb verbal instructions. On one occasion her employer, who wished to send out advertising material, had spent many hours telephoning businesses in person to find out exactly whom he should address his letters to.

He then asked Meg to prepare personalized letters and matching envelopes ready to be sent out. He asked her to be sure that the name on the letter matched the name on the envelope. He then left for a lunch appointment. Returning by chance to the office to pick up something he had forgotten, he found Meg stuffing the envelopes randomly – she had not taken in the last part of his instructions. Having on this occasion narrowly avoided a public relations disaster, Meg's boss learnt to check carefully in future that all his instructions had been understood.

In general, in an office environment, it is good to give instructions in writing as well as verbally – for example, they could be e-mailed to an employee. Alternatively, the employee could use a voice recorder to record the instructions so that he could listen to them carefully later. If instructions have to be given verbally, then it is important for the manager to speak slowly, to leave a pause between instructions which are part of a sequence, and finally to check back that the instructions have been understood.

It is particularly helpful to give clear and precise instructions about how to use various machines in the office. For example:

- Above the photocopier and printer put typed lists of instructions in colour with bullet points clearly showing how to use the machines.
- Demonstrate the machines to the employee, and then ask him to do some basic tasks on the machine while you are keeping an eye on him.

Particular care needs to be exercised if a dyspraxic employee goes on a training course. If he receives IT training, for example, it is best if the person who delivers the IT training is knowledgeable about dyspraxia. The sessions should be short to avoid fatigue (1 hour is recommended), and there should be an opportunity to practise what has been learnt from the session immediately after the session.

Other reasonable adjustments on a training course would be

- providing training course material in advance so that the employee can go over this before the course;
- allowing extra time on courses – a short course could be repeated;
- allowing 25% extra time in any tests or examinations.

(For more advice on how training should be conducted, see page 43.)

Speaking and Writing Skills

Many dyspraxic people find it hard to organize spoken and written communication, and this adversely affects efficiency at work.

Poor organization of speech can result in rambling monologues, verbosity, repetition, hesitation, and long pauses. Poor organization of writing leads to poorly structured written work and the need to spend a long time reorganizing and correcting what has been written. There can be a tendency to spend time getting the detail right whilst losing sight of the overall picture. Hours can be wasted that, with better planning, could have been used for more productive work. The following two scenarios give examples of how dyspraxic employees can be helped by the provision of appropriate reasonable adjustments.

Speaking skills

Ann, a PA to a Vice President in a consulting firm, found it difficult to put her thoughts succinctly into words. She was constantly rambling off the point. Her boss noticed her confusion and asked me to give her some help in improving her oral skills.

I advised her to make good notes before meetings – these notes would not just be a list of questions, but would begin with no more than three targets or aims she had for the meeting, followed by a list of points she wished to make in order to achieve these aims.

Ann practised this a few times with me and found it so successful that she began to use this method for all her meetings, even sometimes for informal meetings with friends. She found it particularly useful when she was speaking on the telephone, and communication was reliant on speech alone rather than a mix of speech and body language. Having a good strategy also made her more confident. Previously on the telephone, if she had been asked a question and could not immediately answer, she had become flustered; now she was able to stay calm and tell the client that she did not have the answer immediately but would ring back or e-mail with the information. (She said she sometimes felt she was rehearsing her points in the same way as comedians rehearse their jokes.) She found that a small amount of preparation vastly improved her communication skills.

Structuring written work

Grant worked as an event organizer for a large Edinburgh company. He was dyspraxic and found it difficult to organize written work. He had difficulty in seeing the overall aim of the projects he worked on and tended to spend time on unnecessary details. He spent many hours writing and, to keep up with his workload, would often stay late in the office. This led to him becoming tired and stressed and his efficiency suffered.

His manager showed him how to use mind maps to plan his work and this helped Grant to see the overall structure of a project at a glance and to work logically through the detailed issues while not losing sight of the main point. It also enabled him to work on several projects at the same time without getting confused. Initially he made his own mind maps, but eventually moved on to using the software mind-mapping programme, MindManager.

Work Organization

Efficiency in the workplace crucially depends on being well organized: knowing what has to be done, by which date it should be done, what steps or stages are involved in doing it, where relevant materials (e.g. files) are located, and so on. Many people who had developed reasonably good organizational skills when they were at college or university can find themselves floundering when they enter the workplace.

Rebecca, a 23-year-old graduate in modern languages was keen to prove herself in her new job in advertising. Although she had had some difficulties at college, she had been able to learn good study skills and had done well in her degree. She therefore did not anticipate having major problems in the workplace. For the first month, as she learnt her new role, she managed reasonably well, and she also had the constant support of her manager.

However, after this initial period, as Rebecca's workload increased and she was asked to work more independently, things started to go wrong: she found she was missing deadlines, forgetting appointments, and being late for work. She was unable to organize a coherent work schedule, and as papers piled up on her desk, she increasingly lost track of things, and almost came to dread going into the office. She found it quite humiliating that she was unable to master her new responsibilities, and was fearful that she would not be able to keep her job.

Rebecca's manager realized that he would have to 'take her in hand'. After seeking advice from a dyspraxia tutor, he worked out a new routine with Rebecca which was designed to train her in orderly habits. The components of the routine were as follows:

- Rebecca bought two new alarm clocks with loud rings, and set one to go off 15 min after the other to ensure that she got up in the morning and left home by 8.15 a.m. prompt.

- On three days of each week (Monday, Wednesday, and Friday) Rebecca had a breakfast meeting with her manager to help ensure that she did arrive on time at the office. This meeting also enabled her to plan her day carefully with the manager and so get into the habit of thinking through what work needed to be done and scheduling it in a practicable way.
- Rebecca was given a whole day free of work to clear her desk and sort her paper and computer files. Her manager helped her to set up filing systems and to allocate trays for urgent and pending work which were always clearly visible on her desk. Rebecca also placed a small plastic basket on the desk as a repository for things she was continually losing, such as her mobile phone, diary, and so on.
- Her manager advised her to spend 10 minutes at the beginning of each morning sorting out the papers and files she would need during the day. In this way, she began her working day with everything in order, and knowing where everything was.
- Her manager held a copy of her diary and for the first week reminded her to leave enough time to arrive early for her appointments.
- Monthly supervision meetings were changed to weekly supervision meetings to set action points for the week ahead.

Once these new routines had been established, Rebecca was gradually able to acquire better habits and she felt much more confident about coping with her workload. Tasks did not seem so daunting once they had been broken down into short stages, and these stages linked with action points.

After a few weeks of acquiring the habits of good organization and planning, Rebecca was able to work independently and confidently. There were occasions when her good habits slipped, and perhaps her desk descended into its old chaos, but her manager was able to monitor this and 'give her a nudge' to get her back on track. In a short time Rebecca's organizational skills became second nature to her.

Sensitivity to Noise, Light, and Movement

Many dyspraxic people are easily distracted by noise or movement, and find bright light disturbing. An example:

Tim, a dyspraxic trainee accountant, who was sensitive to noise and light, worked in a large open-plan office and found his office environment very disturbing. The room had low ceilings and harsh fluorescent lighting. The desks were arranged in rows and Tim was placed in the middle of a row with colleagues at either side of him. Not only did he find it difficult to use his speech recognition software because of the noise around him but he found the general office noise overwhelming. He disliked sensing movement behind him and would constantly turn round to see what was going on. He was also easily distracted by other people talking on the telephone, and generally found it difficult to concentrate. He became very tired after working for a few hours in this office, and his work and health suffered.

Tim's manager tried to find ways to help him. First he offered Tim some noise cancelling headphones so that he could work undisturbed by surrounding noise. However, Tim was still distracted by movement. His manager then decided to set Tim's desk apart from the others in a corner of the office with filing cabinets providing a screen so that Tim had a calmer area in which to work. He was encouraged to place a DO NOT DISTURB notice on the filing cabinets if he was doing work that needed particular concentration. The manager also allowed Tim to use a meeting room when this was free – this room did not have fluorescent lighting and so was altogether a more relaxing environment for Tim to work in.

Emotional Difficulties and Stress

Dyspraxic people, like their dyslexic counterparts, frequently suffer from stress and emotional distress, and this has a detrimental effect on both their personal life and their work performance. The whole area of stress, emotions, and attitudes is dealt with in detail in Chapter 10. Sufficient to say here that it is helpful for managers to keep themselves informed about the emotional aspects of dyspraxic difficulties and of the way these impact on work performance.

They can also take care not to become impatient with someone who they feel is not catching on quickly enough. For example, a line manager who is a rapid thinker and fluent talker may find a dyspraxic employee maddeningly slow on the uptake. A dyspraxia-aware manager, however, will realize that it is his/her responsibility to talk a little more slowly rather than expecting the dyspraxic person to magically speed up their information-processing skills.

Conclusion

Like everyone else, dyspraxic people have both strengths and weaknesses. There are perhaps some jobs that dyspraxic people will not want to attempt. For example, if they are extremely clumsy, then perhaps they should not aspire to be brain surgeons; if they have poor judgement of space, then maybe they should put aside their ambitions to be golf champions and just enjoy the game at whatever level they can play it. However, with a sensible career choice, sympathetic help, good strategies, and IT support, a dyspraxic person can make a success of almost any job. (See page 158 for where to obtain career advice.)

Many famous dyslexic people have recently ‘come out of the closet’ to show that dyslexia is not a bar to success; perhaps it is now time for more dyspraxic celebrities to make themselves known to the public and to show that dyspraxia too is no barrier to achievement.

INFORMATION POINT D

Neurodiversity

David Grant

The term neurodiversity is a recent one: it was first used in 1998 as a positive way of describing autistics. Within a couple of years it was adopted by other groups of individuals whose difficulties include:

- Dyslexia.
- Dyspraxia.
- Attention Deficit Disorder.
- Attention Deficit Hyperactivity Disorder.
- Autism/Asperger's Syndrome.
- Nonverbal learning disorder.
- Dyscalculia.

People with the above specific learning differences have come together to form DANDA (Developmental Adult Neuro-Diversity Association).

The concept of neurodiversity has two key elements. Firstly, it refers to the fact that there is a group of people whose brains are 'wired' differently from 'neurotypicals' (people who do not have the learning differences listed above). Secondly, it is seen as being a positive statement of being different. A person who states that they are neurodiverse is saying: 'I am different but I want to be accepted for what I am, and not be seen as failing to be what you would like, or imagine me to be.'

Two atypical perceptual abilities can also be put under the neurodiversity label:

- Synaesthesia.
- Visualization.

Dyslexia and Employment Edited by Sylvia Moody
© 2009 John Wiley & Sons, Ltd

Dyslexia and dyspraxia have been covered in detail in other chapters in this book, so in this short 'information sheet' chapter, I shall give information about the other seven types of learning difference listed above.

Attention Deficit Disorder (ADD)

Whilst most people will at certain times experience concentration lapses and a tendency to distractibility, ADDers (which is how people with ADD describe themselves) experience these problems more frequently and severely.

Although ADDers are able to maintain concentration when doing a task which interests or challenges them, they can easily go 'off-task' and so time management can be a problem. ADDers may, therefore, find office routines difficult, but may do well in jobs where they only have to perform tasks and/or deal with people for a short period of time, for example in bar or retail work.

Lengthy written tasks, such as report writing or project management – both of which require forward planning – would certainly be difficult for ADDers, as they would find themselves overwhelmed with ideas and not know which ideas to select or what order to put them in. As regards general work organization, ADDers, who tend to be visually oriented, could be helped by colour coding of files and diaries.

Attention Deficit Hyperactivity Disorder (ADHD)

This is a variant of ADD. In addition to suffering lapses in concentration, ADDers with hyperactivity are often also restless and impulsive – they seem to have an excess of energy and need to be constantly moving around. Consequently, they may need to exercise daily, unless they are in a job that requires physical activity. A desk job will present a challenge to them, and also probably to their colleagues who may be distracted by their constant fidgeting and habit of sighing or muttering to themselves.

Autism/Asperger's Syndrome

Autism in general is characterized by difficulties with forming and maintaining social relationships, a lack of empathy, an obsession with detail, and a liking for inflexible routines. When this collection of traits is present in a relatively mild form, Asperger's Syndrome is often the appropriate diagnosis. Some autistics prefer to describe themselves as Aspies.

By the time they have entered employment, many Aspies will have learnt some basic social skills and will be aware of their own strengths and weaknesses in respect of these. They will, nevertheless, benefit from staff development sessions that focus on team building and contributing to/conducting meetings. In general, they appear to thrive in employment that requires great attention to detail, for example, in a work environment that is scientific or mechanical rather than social.

Nonverbal Learning Disorder, Sometimes also Known as Right Hemisphere Dysfunction

This is best thought of as an imbalance between the right and left sides of the brain with language skills being much better than visual ability. The weakness in visual skills may sometimes give rise to mild signs of Asperger's and dyspraxia: face recognition can be weak, and the learning of a layout of a building, for example, a large office building, can take a longer than usual time.

Dyscalculia

Dyscalculia may be described as an inability to grasp basic mathematical concepts. In its 'pure' form it manifests itself as a lack of a sense of proportionality, that is an inability to distinguish 'more than' from 'less than'. For example, if told that Ravi's bonus is 15%, John's is 12%, and Rosie's is 18%, an individual with a pure form of dyscalculia will be unable to say who received the biggest bonus and who received the smallest. This pure form of dyscalculia is very rare.

For other forms of mathematical difficulty, the phrase 'specific maths difficulty' is more useful than the term 'dyscalculia', as the former focuses attention on the specific form of the difficulty. Some people who excel at some types of mathematics, for example, algebra, calculus, and matrices, find other very simple types of maths, such as mental arithmetic, difficult. However, a difficulty with mental arithmetic can often be more usefully related to a dyslexic difficulty (poor short-term memory) than being given the dyscalculia label. Other difficulties with numbers which people often report, such as misreading or reversing numbers, are also probably dyslexic in nature.

For these reasons, to 'bundle' all types of mathematical difficulty under the label 'dyscalculia', is misleading and uninformative – the specific nature of the difficulties needs to be described in detail, and consideration given to whether the cause of these could be dyslexia or dyspraxia, or whether it is truly a pure mathematical difficulty.

In the workplace, individuals who experience difficulties with mental arithmetic can rely on calculators and electronic tills. Individuals who have pure dyscalculia may, in spite of good teaching, never understand certain maths concepts. While they can be taught to carry out maths procedures, they are unlikely to spot mistakes. It might be wiser for such individuals to avoid jobs which require careful and rapid calculations to be done.

Synaesthesia

Synaesthesia occurs when one sense modality, for example, hearing, automatically triggers off another sense modality, for example, vision. For example, when a synaesthesic person hears a musical note, they may simultaneously see a flash of colour. Or when they hear, for example, the word 'Monday', they might immediately experience a brief yellow sensation, while 'Tuesday' might trigger a brief green sensation.

Synaesthesia is much more common than most people realize: about one in 25 people are synaesthetes. For many it is felt to be an enriching experience. In the workplace, it can be helpful with work organization, as some synaesthetes see the names of, for example, projects, files, days, and months in colour. On rare occasions, however, the degree of synaesthesia can be so extreme that sensory overload can occur and this can interfere with reading for comprehension or listening to a conversation.

Visualization

Visualization refers to the ability to create visual images and to keep these 'in the minds eye'. So it could include the ability to read a story, a set of instructions or a procedure, and to simultaneously 'see' these in considerable detail. It also includes the ability to 'see' words simultaneously as words and images, and this can greatly aid spelling. It could also enable, say, a sales representative to remember a route after just one journey, or it could enable someone in the media or fashion industry to remember an object or image after having seen it just once – a particular advantage for buyers.

A strong visualization ability may sometimes mask a weak auditory working memory, and so, while visualizers can perform well in tasks in which they can use their visual strength, they may be weak at other tasks which rely on auditory memory – for example, remembering people's names.

It may be noted that most synaesthetes and visualizers are unaware that their sensory experiences are in any way different from those of other people.

Useful Web Sites

www.ADHD.org.uk
www.DANDA.org.uk

Organizations

National Autistic Society www.nas.org.uk (has a page specifically for employers).
UK Synaesthesia Association www.brighton-breezy.co.uk.

CHAPTER 6

How To Do an Assistive Technology Assessment*

Sylvia Moody

Assistive technology (AT) is an important – often a vital – component of a support package for dyslexic employees. The term 'assistive technology' covers both IT equipment, for example, laptop, software programs, and helpful 'gadgets', for example, ergonomic keyboard.

In order to determine the precise AT needs of an employee in a particular job, a specialist assessment must be done. And in order to ensure that the AT is used effectively, training needs to be carried out in a way that dyslexic employees find helpful. In this chapter, I shall give advice on good practice in assessment, writing an AT needs report, and training.

Assessment

When a dyslexic employee seeks help and support for their workplace difficulties, they will – ideally – be referred for a comprehensive assessment which has the following three components:

- Diagnostic dyslexia assessment.
- Workplace Needs assessment.
- Specialist AT needs assessment.

These three assessments progressively narrow down the focus of investigation. The first looks at whether dyslexia (or some other specific

*The author acknowledges helpful advice on this article from Susan Close, IT Consultant.

Dyslexia and Employment Edited by Sylvia Moody
© 2009 John Wiley & Sons, Ltd

learning difficulty) is present; the second looks at how the dyslexic difficulties affect workplace efficiency and makes *general* recommendations for workplace skills training and AT support; the third is a more specialist AT assessment. It should be emphasized that AT support should always be combined with a workplace skills training programme.

In carrying out the specialist AT assessment, the assessor should:

1. *Check core computer skills.* Before beginning any IT training, it is vital to check if the employee has mastered basic computer skills. Some clients may have little idea of how to create and copy files, cut and paste, and so on. If this is the case, it is necessary to go one step back and teach the employee these skills before moving on to teach particular software programs.

   It may be noted here that, if an application is made to Access to Work (AtW) for help with funding the training, AtW will only be prepared to fund training in IT, not in core computer skills. However, employers are sometimes willing to fund the core skills training themselves.
2. *Consider specific job requirements.* It is *not* useful to make general or vague recommendations, such as the following:

   > The client should be provided with voice-recognition and text-to-speech software, and also mind-mapping software for organising thoughts.

   Equally unhelpful is to simply give a list of specific software items, for example, TextHelp, Dragon, without explaining their use. It is important to explain exactly why you have recommended particular pieces of equipment, that is, making clear the specific ways in which this equipment can be helpful to a client in his particular job. (In this chapter, masculine pronouns refer to the client, feminine pronouns to the assessor/trainer.)

   For example, it is of little use recommending Dragon if the employee has to input data which consists of long complex codes or complicated foreign addresses. It would probably be more useful to recommend a touch-typing course and training in good proofreading skills.
3. *Select specific components of the software programs which are useful.* It may not be necessary to teach a client everything about, say, TextHelp, as only selected parts of this programme may be useful in a specific case.

4. *If possible, demonstrate the programs using real work tasks.* It may be that the employee is simultaneously working with a dyslexia trainer to improve efficiency in work tasks, and, in this case, it may be possible to work on the same material that the dyslexia trainer is using.
5. *Take account of the client's general skills, in particular the significant strengths or weaknesses in his performance, and also his learning style.* A dyslexic client may have a poor short-term memory, and consequently will have difficulty in remembering a series of instructions or correctly carrying out a sequence of movements. Also, he will quickly tire if he is asked to absorb large amounts of complex information. This may make him slower than the average person in mastering sequences of computer commands.

   If the client has poor listening skills, he may not be able to 'frame' text in his mind in a series of sentences, clauses, and so on, and so may have difficulty using a voice-to-text programme, such as Dragon. If he has poor fine motor control, he may not have the skills to use the particular interface style of a mind-mapping program.
6. *Allow extra time for training.* It may be necessary to allow a client extra time for training on software programs. For example, a half-day of training on Dragon would probably be inadequate – at least a day's training would be needed if this programme were to be used with a reasonable degree of confidence and efficiency. If insufficient or inadequate training is given, and the employee fails to learn the programs, this could be wrongly interpreted by managers as evidence that the employee is uncooperative or unmotivated.

How to Write an AT Needs Report

In this section, I shall suggest a format for an AT assessment report. After giving an overall structure for the report, I shall use the fictional case of Andrew Bennett, a civil servant, to illustrate the content of the various sections of the report.

Structure of the report

Referral
Background

Previous report(s)
Interviews with Mr Bennett and his line manager
Recommendations for equipment
Recommendations for training
Further information
Review of progress
Prices and suppliers

Content of the report

Referral

Here you describe Mr Bennett's job and explain who has made the referral and why.

> Mr Bennett, a junior civil servant, was referred for an AT assessment by his line manager, James Griffiths, because of concerns that he was inefficient in some aspects of his work.

Background

In this section, you give more detail about Mr Bennett's job, and report *separately* information received from Mr Bennett himself about his strengths and difficulties, and information supplied by his line manager. For example:

> Mr Bennett's job involves doing a large amount of reading for research purposes and writing lengthy reports. He also has to liase with a number of outside agencies and frequently has to attend meetings, at some of which he is responsible for taking Minutes. He works from home at least one day a week.
>
> According to his line manager, Mr Griffiths, Mr Bennett's main problem is that he appears to be generally disorganised.
>
> Mr Bennett himself reported that he generally had no difficulties with reading and writing. However, he sometimes found it visually stressful to look at a computer screen for a long period, and he suffered manual fatigue if he had to type for lengthy periods. He felt that his main difficulties were problems with memory and organisational skills. He said that he often lost files or important papers, and turned up at meetings with the wrong set of documents. He had difficulty with note- and Minute-taking, and sometimes forgot or became muddled about instructions he had been given. He tried to organise himself by making notes about things he should be doing, but then tended to lose the notes.

Previous report(s)

Here you can summarize the results of any previous dyslexia or Workplace Needs assessment reports, and, if available, reports of work reviews:

> Mr Bennett has recently had a diagnostic assessment. According to the assessment report, his general intellectual ability is very high, but he has weaknesses in auditory short-term memory and visual tracking. His phonological skills are also relatively poor, but he has compensated well for this and there are no significant weaknesses in his general literacy skills.

Interviews with Mr Bennett and his line manager

> I interviewed Mr Bennett at his workplace on 22nd July 2008. His line manager, James Griffiths, was also present. The purpose of this meeting was to
>
> - ascertain what hardware and software packages were in use;
> - discuss Mr Bennett's strengths and difficulties;
> - assess training requirements;
> - appraise workplace conditions.
>
> Mr Bennett was extremely co-operative throughout the consultation and seemed well-motivated to learn new skills.
>
> A second meeting with Mr Bennett took place on 13th October 2008 at my premises. The purpose of this meeting was to discuss possible AT aids that I considered appropriate for Mr Bennett and to give him a demonstration of these tools. This allowed Mr Bennett to see if he felt comfortable using various software items.

Recommendations for equipment

It is important to give a detailed justification of your reasons for recommending particular items of equipment. For example:

> 1. *Personal digital assistant* (*PDA*). Mr Bennett is frequently away from his office attending meetings, and he also regularly works from home. He currently carries printed-out information sheets with him. A PDA would allow him to have all his contact details (e-mails, telephone numbers, etc.) to hand at all times when he is out of the office. It would also allow him to have electronic files

(surveys, reports, agenda, Minutes of meetings) instantly available for reference.

Mr Bennett also reports that he sometimes has difficulty in remembering what to do and when to do it. A PDA which was synchronised with his PC at work would make him far more efficient at, for example, scheduling and remembering appointments.

2. *Digital voice recorder*. A digital voice recorder would act as a 'memory back-up' for Mr Bennett. He could use it to record meetings, important conversations (provided confidentiality was not an issue) and instructions. He could also use it to give himself reminders about things he needed to do, or to 'capture' passing thoughts which it might be useful for him to remember at a later date.
3. *Screen ruler*. A screen ruler would relieve the visual stress which Mr Bennett suffers when he works for long periods at the computer. The ruler provides support to readers who find it difficult to track text across the screen, and assists them in viewing text or tables of figures. Fully adjustable, it provides a 'strip' or 'ruler' across the screen with control over magnification or contrast. The background can be 'greyed' or dimmed out as desired and the cursor colour can also be changed easily. The screen ruler will work with most pieces of software as it acts as an 'overlay' on the PC screen.
4. *Ergonomic keyboard*. As Mr Bennett suffers manual fatigue when he types for lengthy periods, he may find it more comfortable to use an ergonomic keyboard with his PC, and, whenever possible, to use a full-size wireless keyboard with his laptop. He would also benefit from using wrist supports.

At the end of each of these sections, you need to make a specific recommendation for the item of equipment recommended and give the number of training hours that will be needed for it.

Recommendations for training

The trainer must be experienced in teaching IT to people with dyslexia and/or dyspraxia.

Mr Bennett should be given one-to-one tutorials that are delivered in sessions not exceeding two hours' in duration, and with regular breaks (every 40 minutes if sitting at a VDU, less often if the training sessions includes tasks which are not done on a computer).

The trainer should tailor the lesson content to the requirements of Mr Bennett's job, rather than explaining everything the software has to offer.

Further information: accessibility options

Many accessibility features are built into Microsoft and other similar software. These include: keyboard shortcuts, size and zoom options, toolbar, menu and sound options, screen colour combinations. Accessibility features can help reduce key strokes and automate repetitive tasks – using, for example, Autotext, Autocorrect, and Styles and Formatting. It will also be useful for Mr Bennett to experiment with using different fonts to see which he finds easiest to read.

Review of progress

Mr Bennett's progress should be reviewed in six months' time when further support and/or tools may be appropriate.

Prices and suppliers

This section should include recommended supplier details and quotes for hardware, software, delivery, installation, and training.

INFORMATION POINT E

Visual Stress

Melanie Jameson

What Is Visual Stress?

The term *Visual Stress* refers to a range of symptoms experienced during reading, even though the eyes appear to be functioning normally. The symptoms include

- frequently losing the place in a text;
- seeing white paper as 'glaring';
- headaches and eye strain;
- perceiving the print as becoming blurred or floating off the page;
- seeing a shadowy outline round the words;
- perceiving the words as appearing to join up, leaving no spaces in-between;
- perceiving the spaces between words as a river of white, running down the page, drawing attention away from the words.

Confusingly, this condition has formerly also been known by the following names:

Scotopic Sensitivity Syndrome.
Visual Discomfort.
Meares–Irlen Syndrome.

Dyslexia and Employment Edited by Sylvia Moody
© 2009 John Wiley & Sons, Ltd

How does Visual Stress Link with Dyslexia?

Sometimes these visual difficulties can be traced to undetected eye problems. Research has established that people with dyslexia are prone to certain types of visual dysfunction, in particular impaired binocular function (when the eyes do not work effectively together); poor focusing across a range of distances (needed when switching between the blackboard/whiteboard and notetaking); and low reserves of eye muscle capacity. Irregular eye movements and poor tracking across the page have also been highlighted as key areas of difficulty.

A further visual handicap is 'pattern glare'; this describes the way in which certain patterns, including lines of print, become unpleasant to look at, causing illusions of colour, shape, and motion.

It is not suggested that these visual factors are the *cause* of dyslexia – dyslexia is known to have complex neurological origins – but they can contribute considerably to the difficulties experienced with reading, both at the early stage of mastering literacy and later in reading fluently and automatically with full comprehension.

The Jameson Visual Stress Checklist, developed in partnership with the Institute of Optometry, is shown in Appendix I. It highlights symptoms of visual stress and indicates if specialist intervention is required.

Difficulties in the Workplace

Visual stress can reduce a competent employee to the level of a word-by-word reader, unable to skim through or scan documentation. Following lines of digits can be equally challenging. There is a particular sensitivity to any form of glare or flicker; these effects can be caused by fluorescent lighting in the office, publications on glossy paper, and computer screens. The last mentioned is of special concern, given the amount of time many workers spend on their computers. The effort that goes into reading may result in headaches and unpleasant symptoms such as dry itchy eyes.

Approaches to Treatment

It is recommended that everyone with visual stress should have an eye examination by an optometrist specializing in this area. (A link to a web site listing relevant specialists is given at the end of this chapter.) The examination should be free for children at school and in full-time education up to age of 19. Eye exercises, drops, or spectacles may be prescribed.

If problems remain, the optometrist may recommend coloured filters, that is, coloured overlays or tinted spectacle lenses. The best shade for spectacle lenses is generally found by using a piece of equipment called a *Colorimeter*, which displays text illuminated by different colours. (A charge is made for a colorimetry assessment.) Other approaches, such as orthoscopics, may be used.

It is not only people with dyslexia who suffer from visual stress. Work in this area was first undertaken to help sufferers from migraine and epilepsy. Both groups can find that certain shapes, or the effect of black print on white paper, can form unpleasant patterns and bring on attacks. The use of tints – either coloured overlays or tinted spectacles – seemed to prevent hypersensitive areas in the brain from over-reacting. Since some people with dyslexia also experienced a glare or other indications of visual stress, it was logical to investigate whether colour could also assist this group.

A specialist optometric assessment, followed by precise application of colour therapy, is the only treatment approach recommended by the Institute of Optometry. A number of other interventions are available, namely: Irlen lenses, Behavioural Optometry, and Orthoscopics.

Colour Therapy

There is concern that the availability of overlays to non-eye care professionals (such as tutors) leads to the risk of them being 'prescribed' without investigation of visual dysfunction. For that reason the Institute of Optometry has made the following statement:

> A thorough eye examination should always be carried out with particular attention to the ophthalmic correlates of dyslexia.

Furthermore, the Institute points out that some types of eye problems will require the involvement of other specialists: an Orthoptist (who specializes in the function of the eye muscles) or an

Ophthalmologist (an eye consultant trained in medical/surgical treatment of eye diseases).

Unfortunately, the cost of a specialist visual assessment and/or the unavailability of practitioners with this expertise (e.g. in prisons) may lead to overlays being handed out as the only remediation.

Indicators that colour therapy might be beneficial:

- Symptoms of visual stress/persistent eye strain despite conventional eye treatment.
- Dyslexia (once ocular correction has been attended to).
- Headaches or migraine in the family.
- Photosensitive epilepsy.

Assistance for University Students

At the time of going to press, the Department for Innovation, Universities and Skills (DIUS) is considering recommendations for the costs of visual and colorimetry assessments to be met by the Disabled Students' Allowance.

Good Practice

Ease of deciphering print is significantly affected by the nature of the reading material being scanned: difficulties are exacerbated by small print, badly spaced text, bright white paper, and the use of 'fancy' fonts and 'busy' backgrounds. Text should be left justified *only*: this makes it easier for the reader to keep his/her place on the page when transferring from one line to the next, and largely prevents the illusion of rivulets of white meandering down the page.

Self-Help Strategies

The following self-help advice should be given to those who are prone to visual stress:

- Use 'natural' light bulbs in desk lamps with a wide enough arc to spread light evenly over the desk.
- Wear a peaked cap to reduce glare from bright neon lights.
- Use a TNT computer screen (flat screen) which has less flicker.
- Modify fore- and background colours on your computer according to which colours you find easy on the eye.
- Enlarge fonts when reading from the computer and/or when printing off material.
- If text is level down both margins, change to left-justification where possible – for example, scan into a computer and modify before reading.
- Buy tinted A4 lined pads for writing.
- When studying a written text, photocopy or print it off on tinted paper. Often pale blue-grey is best for personal use. It is economical to buy this by the ream, and this also enables you to give supplies of it to other people, for example, trainers, who produce handouts or other material that you will need to read.

To conclude, the very acquisition of literacy can be jeopardized if symptoms arising from visual stress are untreated. Conversely, the successful identification and treatment of visual stress can lead to a dramatic improvement in not only reading but also handwriting, spelling, and even hand/eye coordination and spatial abilities. All professionals who screen, assess, or support people with dyslexia are strongly urged to check for visual stress and to provide appropriate guidance.

Summary

1. Visual stress with or without undetected eye problems may be a factor in failure to read efficiently.
2. A routine eye test may not always detect the types of visual dysfunction referred to above in this article.
3. Visual stress is experienced not only by dyslexic people, but also by migraine and epilepsy sufferers.
4. Visual stress is exacerbated by small-sized fonts and poorly spaced text.

Web Sites Listing Specialist Eye-Care Practitioners

www.ceriumvistech.co.uk
www.s4clp.org

Further Information

www.essex.ac.uk/psychology/overlays

CHAPTER 7

Disputes around Dyslexia

Katherine Kindersley

Disputes at work are costly and to be avoided. They interfere with work performance and productivity. They are time consuming and emotionally draining for all the parties involved. They are unlikely to promote an organization's image and may bring adverse publicity, particularly if they reach the stage of an employment tribunal.

In this chapter, I shall look at disputes which have their origin in dyslexic difficulties and the way these difficulties are managed in the workplace. I shall be drawing on my own experience as a workplace dyslexia consultant to give illustrations of how disputes can arise and of ways in which a consultant can try to resolve them by working with all the stakeholders in the case: the dyslexic employee, managers, and other professional groups who may be involved.

Causes of Disputes

The particular causes of disputes around dyslexia can be as varied as the world of employment itself. Consider the variables in any given situation: the workplace environment, the range of operational and management styles, the complex mix of individual personalities working alongside one another, the work and organizational culture. Fertile ground, one would think, for many diverse conflicts to arise. Yet experience shows that most conflicts in the workplace have certain underlying themes in common. If these themes are recognized, then timely action can be taken to prevent the conflicts turning into disputes. In this

Dyslexia and Employment Edited by Sylvia Moody
© 2009 John Wiley & Sons, Ltd

chapter, I will be concerned in particular with the theme of change in the workplace, as this can lead to disputes in a number of ways.

Change as a Cause of Disputes

The following are examples of changes in the workplace which may adversely affect the work performance and/or the emotional well-being of a dyslexic employee: (In the sections of this chapter which are not part of a case study, masculine pronouns refer to the employee, feminine pronouns to the manager.)

Promotion

Promotion is not always good news for a dyslexic employee. It may mean that he has new responsibilities which he finds daunting and which may lead to a drop in his performance levels. For example, an employee who, in his previous position had excelled in good practical problem solving and communication skills, finds himself promoted to a role which makes increased demands on literacy. He may be required to keep meticulous written records, manage his own correspondence, and write reports. He soon realizes that he does not have the requisite skills.

Style of management

As a result of re-structuring, there is a new team manager. She introduces a very different style of management which is less sympathetic to a dyslexic employee. This leads to clashes with the employee, who has been accustomed to doing his job in a particular way and finds change difficult. Perhaps he has been taking work home, working longer hours, or avoiding a task or activity altogether.

Change in appraisal systems

New appraisal systems may record performance in a more detailed way. The employee may be required to produce more in the way of documentation and there can be greater monitoring and supervision, which highlights weak performance.

Loss of a support system

A particularly supportive colleague has moved on – for example, the secretary who was willing to proofread all the e-mails and documents before they were sent out. Or it can be that the end of a relationship at home has left the employee with no one to check over written documents.

Case Study 1: Over-Promoted?

How promotion cost a promising market research assistant her job

I received a telephone call from an HR Officer at Wealth Management and Analysis, a financial products company involved in market research. The company wanted a diagnostic and Workplace Needs assessment for an employee called Sophie, who worked as a research assistant.

Background

I began to collect appropriate documentation. From this I learned that Sophie was in the Second Review stage of the Capability procedure and was apparently about to lose her job. The reports from the Second Capability Interview stated that she had failed to improve her performance and to meet the targets set by her line manager in the First Capability Review Interview. A letter stated that she had 4 weeks in which to meet these targets. The most serious concern was the quality of her writing and her slowness in producing reports.

Sophie's line manager, Martin, sent me a memorandum in which he gave me further background information. In this he explained that Sophie had been promoted from the Pension Fund team to a position in his department, Equity Investments. Previous work appraisals had indicated that she was bright and able to absorb new information quickly. In client presentations, she engaged readily with her audience and responded well to questions. At meetings she invariably made valuable contributions. In the interview for her present position, she had seemed promising. She had gained a good understanding of equity-based investment products and was able to talk about these in an articulate and knowledgeable way. Her new position differed from her previous one in that she now had to produce much more in the way of written work: lengthy and detailed reports on a range of stocks and securities for the Private Equity team.

Meeting with Martin, the line manager

I arranged a meeting with Martin to gain a clearer understanding of his perspective. To illustrate his concerns, Martin showed me one of Sophie's draft reports, pointing out that it lacked a clear structure and contained many careless errors of spelling and grammar, as well as inaccurate facts. He also showed me a diary of dated entries where Sophie's work had been sub-standard, and he expressed great irritation about this. He added that another difficulty was her interaction with her colleagues. He had received complaints that she constantly muttered under her breath when reading, interrupting other people in their work.

I asked whether the demand for good writing skills in this new job had been made clear at the interview stage, or whether there had been any assessment of her writing ability. Martin said no – he had assumed that Sophie's skills would have been assessed when she was first appointed to the company, and that, as she had a university degree, she should be able to write accurately.

I said that I would be assessing Sophie for dyslexia in a week's time and, in the circumstances, it was inappropriate for Martin to continue with the capability procedure.

Comment 1: Capability procedure
Once an employee is referred for a dyslexia assessment, it is inappropriate to continue with capability procedures. Assessment will reveal whether an employee has dyslexia or other specific learning difficulties, and a Workplace Needs assessment will make recommendations for a specialist training programme and other reasonable adjustments. The effect of these interventions should be monitored and a reasonable time allowed for new skills to be gained and secured. Following this, work performance can be assessed.

Assessment of Sophie

In my preliminary discussion with Sophie, she said that she was very worried about the results of the assessment. In fact she was very worried about anything to do with work. She was not sleeping, she suffered what she described as panic attacks while on her way to work in the morning, and sometimes, at work, she felt so frustrated and upset that she had to leave the office and have a good cry on her own. She had desperately wanted to do well in this new job, and felt bewildered as to why she had such problems dealing with paperwork and writing reports. She said her spelling and grammar seemed to be getting worse by the day, and that perhaps this was something to do with feeling so stressed.

She felt very upset in particular by criticism of her writing. She was anxious to get things right and she often spent a great deal of time writing a few paragraphs. She had tried reading her work aloud, muttering the words under her breath, so she could hear some of the mistakes, but she got such glares from colleagues on either side of her that she did not dare continue with this strategy.

I asked her if she thought she was in the right job. She said she thought she had made a mistake. She felt uncomfortable in the office with all the criticism of her work. She said she wavered between being miserable and wanting to leave and feeling resentful and angry. At this point, she broke down in tears and it was some time before she felt calm enough to go ahead with the assessment.

The assessment showed that Sophie was dyslexic, and that her difficulties were mainly with higher level literacy skills, such as reading comprehension and structuring written work. Clearly she had successfully compensated for these difficulties at university and in her previous post, but her present job was highlighting her weaknesses and consequently placing great stress on her. The more anxious and stressed she became, the more inaccurate and illogical she was with her written work.

Comment 2: Selection procedures

It is important that sampling procedures are adopted in the selection process. This ensures that the best candidate for the job is selected, and that the chosen candidate is likely to have the required skills to do the job.

All applicants should be asked to perform the same sample job tasks, selected from the actual range of tasks that the post holder will be expected to do. If required, appropriate reasonable adjustments should be made to prevent discrimination (see Information point B). Performance should be measured against an agreed set of criteria.

In Sophie's case, a writing task would have highlighted the fact that formal writing was not easy for her. Then, given her strong skills in other areas and her good performance record, a decision might have been taken earlier to arrange an assessment for her and to provide appropriate support.

Post-assessment meeting with Martin

I met Martin to discuss with him the results of my assessment and to make various recommendations about Sophie's training needs. I pointed out that it was unreasonable to expect her writing skills to improve in 4 weeks – she would need a longer period of time to learn the relevant skills. I gave details of the individual training programme I would recommend and also of items of assistive technology that would be useful. I also recommended ways in which Martin and other managers could support her.

Martin listened with interest to my recommendations. He said he had not really come across a dyslexic employee before and would be willing to give the training a chance. He also offered to reduce the number of projects Sophie was expected to work on until the training had had a chance to produce results. He did however raise some concerns – and these were typical of the concerns that many managers express in such a situation. He asked how long the process of training would take, the cost of it, and the specific objectives of the training. He also asked if Sophie's skills would be likely to improve sufficiently for her to be able to do the job.

I explained that there was never any guarantee that training would be efficacious – one could only try it and see. I was able to reassure Martin, however, that in the majority of cases, training did enable a dyslexic employee to improve their skills and keep their job. I stressed that liaison between the trainer and line manager was essential to the success of the programme. I also raised the possibility that Sophie might move to an alternative position, perhaps with more client contact where she could use her good spoken communication skills. However, it was agreed that she would continue in her present post for the moment until the results of the training could be assessed.

Comment 3: Efficacy of training
I am often asked about the efficacy of workplace skills training and whether it will enable a dyslexic employee to work to a satisfactory level in the future. There is currently no research in this area and

so we have no reassuring statistics or body of evidence to turn to. Yet my own experience and also that of my colleagues demonstrate that we can be optimistic. Skills training can make *all* the difference. Sometimes progress may seem slow at the beginning, but as skills are built up and secured, as confidence grows and the tensions on both the employee's and the employer's side relax, optimism usually turns out to be justified. However, if assessment reveals a profile of *general* rather than specific learning difficulties, we may be less optimistic. In such cases, progress will be slower, and there may well be other adjustments which need to be made, including a change in job responsibilities.

Helping Sophie

I began the training with Sophie, focussing on improving her writing skills. We started with some help with basic grammar and punctuation which would quickly make a difference to the general impression given by her written work. She made good progress, and I felt that we would soon be ready to move on to higher level writing skills, such as planning and structuring a lengthy text. I had no doubt she would be able to master these skills in a reasonably short time.

However, Sophie continued to be in such a state of stress and anxiety that she was herself unable to appreciate how much improvement she had made. She was frequently tearful in the sessions, and eventually decided that she did not want to continue with the training. She said she had decided that this job was not for her and she was going to hand in her notice. I pointed out that if she applied for another other high-level post, she would again need good writing skills and she now had been given a good opportunity to develop these.

A disappointing outcome

Sophie soldiered on for a few more sessions, but then definitely decided to stop the training and to leave her job. When she spoke to her line manager, Martin, about this, he was disappointed: he had been impressed with the improvement that Sophie's writing had shown during her sessions with me and was now keen to keep her in post. He asked her to reconsider her decision about leaving, but Sophie was adamant. Martin asked me if I could do anything more to persuade her.

I felt caught in a dilemma. I too felt very disappointed that Sophie had decided to hand in her resignation. I felt sure that she did have the ability to gain the writing skills she needed to succeed in her job, and that these skills would serve her well in the future. But should I go on trying to persuade Sophie to change her mind about leaving? Was it ultimately a general lack of confidence and belief in herself that led her to make that decision? Or was the job really too stressful for her? Or was it just a temporary failure of nerve?

I also had to ask myself how far we professionals should go in trying to push clients in a direction which we thought would be 'good for them'. Do we ourselves sometimes feel it is hard to 'let go' of a client and accept that the outcome is not going to be the one that we had anticipated and hoped for? In this case, I felt that I had done all I reasonably could to dissuade Sophie from leaving. She handed in her notice the following week.

General comments

Sophie's case illustrates some important points. Job changes and new responsibilities may prove extremely stressful for the dyslexic employee. I think this is particularly so if the individual has never had a dyslexic assessment and does not understand why some tasks remain so difficult in spite of great effort. Job sampling techniques in the selection process will help to place people in the right job; they may also help to reveal skill areas which need support and training, if the employee is to manage the new position.

When an employee demonstrates uneven performance across different areas of work, perhaps with surprising discrepancies in levels of particular skills, dyslexia may be the cause, and this should be considered before a capability procedure is introduced. I am confident that people with dyslexia, if they are given appropriate training, can gain more efficient and secure skills, even if years of struggle have left them with persistent feelings of low self-esteem and high levels of anxiety.

Case Study 2: A Clash of Personalities

A dyslexic employee who has been 'happy in his work' for 16 years suddenly instigates a grievance procedure when a new line manager is appointed

In this case study, I shall look at a different type of change in the workplace: a change of manager. A dyslexic employee who has coped reasonably well with his job for many years can suddenly find his usual coping strategies and support mechanisms are swept away when a new line manager is appointed.

Background

Robert had worked for 16 years as a structural engineer with SPS Engineers. He had had an assessment when he was at university which had showed him to be dyspraxic. His firm did know about this, but it had never been really discussed. Now, Robert was claiming that he was being unfairly treated and that he was the victim of harassment. He had instigated a grievance procedure.

Observations from the line manager

I was contacted by Madeline, Robert's line manager, and asked to advise on Robert's case. I attended a meeting with Madeline and Carlo, the HR manager, at SPS Engineers.

Carlo acknowledged that Robert had worked for the firm for a long time without difficulties arising. Although he did not know all the details, he had the impression that Robert had previously managed projects satisfactorily, but over the last year, when there had been some changes in management and organization, his performance had significantly declined. He had also become uncharacteristically surly and uncooperative.

Here Madeline joined the discussion abruptly. She claimed that Robert's survival for 16 years was due to the fact that he had never had proper supervision and management. The department had been run in an inefficient and unprofessional way. That was why she had reorganized the work allocation so that engineers were responsible for managing individual projects, instead of, as previously, sharing the responsibility between design teams. She was now able to monitor individual performance.

Carlo agreed with Madeline that, in general, the new arrangements worked better. Most of the engineers had approved of this change as they liked to be in control of their own work from the design stage through to the completion of the job. I asked about Robert's attitude to the change, and Carlo said Robert had not welcomed it: he had complained about the loss of team comradeship, shared knowledge, and collaboration.

Madeline here opined that the truth was that Robert was simply not up to his job. In the past, he had got by through having the help of colleagues who had 'covered' for his inefficiencies. Now that he had to work more independently it was clear that there were many problems with his performance. For example, he often miscalculated figures and was unable to plan schedules, organize outside suppliers, and communicate clearly with draftsmen and technicians. And in general he worked very slowly.

I asked Madeline why she thought Robert had become so difficult and uncooperative, given that he had worked in the firm for 16 years without showing any problems with attitude or behaviour.

Madeline said she thought that Robert was simply upset that his weaknesses had been exposed, and that he was hiding behind this grievance procedure against her. She herself had been willing to offer him extra supervision and had arranged to have his desk moved to a more secluded part of the office so that he could work without interruptions. She denied that she had ever harassed him, and said she was confident that, if the case came to court, it would become evident that all her monitoring and supervision had been necessary and fair.

Observations of the line manager

During the course of the meeting I was conscious of the difference in attitudes to the case between Carlo and Madeline. Carlo was anxious about the situation, but he appeared to think that there could be a negotiable solution, if the right way to help Robert was found; Madeline, by contrast, seemed to have already dismissed Robert as a hopeless case. I had observed during our conversation that Madeline herself was an extremely quick-thinking, rapid-talking person with a brisk, possibly slightly abrasive manner, and I wondered if this might cause a further problem for her relationship with Robert – given that Robert was described as being generally slow in his work.

I asked Madeline how she would describe her general interaction and communication with Robert. She said that, in her supervision sessions with him, she found that he was maddeningly slow to catch on. He would begin a sentence and stop, and so she would finish off his sentence, or move on to the next topic – otherwise they would be there all morning. He tended to contribute little to the discussion himself, and at times seemed bewildered, as if he had not taken in the implications of her comments. She said he tended to behave in the same way at meetings.

She added that another way he was slow was that he liked to produce his drawings by hand. He had explained that this allowed him to see the whole drawing more clearly so that he was able to think about it as he went along. He said that he found computers confusing – the screens were too busy with their profusion of tools.

I pointed out that all the difficulties which Madeline had described, both in working and communication, were characteristic of dyspraxic people, and that Robert could be helped in all these areas. It was then arranged that I carry out an up-to-date diagnostic assessment of Robert, and also do a Workplace Needs assessment. The result of the diagnostic assessment showed that Robert's difficulties were indeed mainly dyspraxic, but that he also had some features of dyslexia and a significant problem with visual stress – the latter made it difficult for him to track numbers and letters on a page or a computer screen. (See Information point E for more information on visual stress.)

Comment 4: Hidden disabilities

An understanding and acceptance of 'hidden' disabilities in the workplace is important. Although the focus here is on dyslexia and dyspraxia, these are not the only hidden disabilities that are present within a workforce. There will be people with other specific learning difficulties such as Attention Deficit Disorder (ADD), Attention Deficit Hyperactivity Disorder (ADHD), Asperger's (social communication difficulties), as well as those affected by mental health conditions, such as stress and depression. There will also be those with medical conditions, such as cancer, multiple sclerosis, and epilepsy, which, in the early stages, or in mild cases, may also be 'hidden'. All of these conditions can impact upon workplace performance, particularly if employers have not adapted their working practices to accommodate the particular needs of their employees.

Conversation with Robert

When I met with Robert to carry out his assessment I asked him to give me his perspective on the current situation. His manner seemed generally depressed, and he appeared somewhat reluctant to talk openly to me about his feelings. However, he did say that from the beginning he had felt that Madeline was hostile to him – she was always hovering over him or checking up on him to see what he was doing, and this made him anxious. Also, without proper consultation, she had moved him into a different part of the office and this made him feel isolated and without support, because previously he had been able to get advice and help from his colleagues if he was unsure about anything. He said he had always managed his job perfectly well in this way, and people were quite happy to help him.

I asked Robert if the organization had given him any training to help him improve his efficiency and get used to new ways of working. He said that he had been sent on one or two training courses, but these had simply multiplied his problems. The sessions had been delivered at a pace that was too quick for him, and in a large group he had not felt able to ask questions. Although the trainers had talked a lot about what to do, they had not actually *shown* him how to do things. When he had returned from the training courses without any improvement in his skills, Madeline had implied that he was unmotivated and uncooperative.

Comment 5: Training courses

Many people with dyslexia do not benefit from training courses in the expected way. They have difficulty in absorbing information from fast-moving spoken presentations, and find they cannot concentrate well for long periods of time, especially if there is a lack of variety in the way that information is being delivered. Robert would have profited more from training courses had adjustments been made for his dyspraxia. For example, he needed to be provided with clearly presented notes and copies of 'PowerPoint' slides in advance – this would have allowed him to become familiar with the material. He might also have been able to mark areas of principle importance, or customize the material visually, perhaps with colours, to make it easier for him to follow.

He would have also found it helpful to repeat one-day courses after a shorter period of time than is usual. In the case of longer courses, he needed the parts of the course to be separated, so that he could have time to process the material from, say, the first two days of the course, before continuing with the rest of the course.

Sometimes adjustments which are useful for dyslexic people can also be useful for all the trainees on a course. Having such adjustments routinely in place obviates the need for a dyslexic employee to disclose his difficulties, if he does not wish to do so.

Post-assessment meeting with Madeline and Carlo

I met again with Carlo and Madeline and told them that my assessment had shown that Robert did indeed have dyspraxic difficulties, but he also had some dyslexic difficulties and a very severe problem with visual stress. I also told them something of my conversation with Robert and the grievances he had mentioned. I explained why he might have felt unsupported and isolated, and that he had possibly been humiliated by the manner in which his desk had been repositioned. I also explained the problems about training courses not taking account of people with dyspraxic or similar difficulties.

In particular, I discussed with Madeline the question of her general communication with Robert, stressing the fact that he could not help being slow in processing information, and that this did not mean that, if given time, he could not find a solution to difficulties or complete projects successfully. I said I felt that, because Robert had felt under pressure during the last year to perform everything quickly, he had become increasingly stressed, and this had set up a vicious circle of poor performance and anxiety each compounding the other.

Carlo and Madeline both showed themselves ready to try to have a better understanding of Robert's difficulties and to find more effective ways of managing him. Madeline acknowledged that she knew nothing about dyspraxia, and that the general impatience she felt with Robert's slowness had probably not helped matters. I then made specific recommendations for a programme of specialist training and IT support for Robert. We also discussed the possibility of arranging an awareness day for managers so that they could have more information about dyspraxia, dyslexia, visual stress, and other related difficulties.

Comment 6: Awareness training

Dyslexia awareness training gives employers the opportunity to gain an understanding of

- how dyslexia and dyspraxia manifest themselves at work;
- how changes in the work environment may impact particularly on employees with 'hidden' disabilities;
- how to develop a best-practice approach to working with colleagues who are dyslexic or dyspraxic.

Workshops and training sessions can be adapted to particular audiences, but they will usually include information on

- the legal framework, including the Disability Discrimination Act and the Data Protection Act;
- intervention and adjustments at all levels: individual, team, and whole organization;
- what 'reasonable adjustments' are usually appropriate;
- how these adjustments can be embedded into policy at all stages of the employment cycle, including recruitment, development and appraisal, promotion, and dismissal;
- specialist workplace skills training programmes;
- Access to Work support and funding.

Outcome

Finally, a meeting was arranged between myself, Carlo, Madeline, and Robert at which we discussed all the issues – and at which Madeline was very careful to give Robert time to finish his sentences! A way of going forward which was satisfactory to everybody was agreed, and at the time of writing, not only is Robert profiting from his training but Madeline is also making equally good progress with her dyspraxia awareness. Robert has been moved back to his old position in the office close to his colleagues and the number of projects for which he is responsible has been reduced. He is becoming more assertive about talking openly about his difficulties to colleagues and managers, expressing his views by e-mail if he finds oral communication difficult. It seems likely that this story will have a happy ending – Robert has dropped his grievance procedure.

General Comments

I come across a good number of cases where a conflict has arisen between colleagues. Perhaps this is not surprising when most people in employment cannot choose their work colleagues or change their managers. Different personalities, different ways of working can easily produce friction. Until Madeleine understood that Robert was not able to speedily organize his thoughts and find the words he needed to express them, she was constantly impatient with him, and consequently she often missed an opportunity to elicit a valuable contribution from him.

In another case, an employee with dyspraxia had her probation period extended by 6 months because she missed meetings and was sometimes late for appointments. She felt hassled by her line manager, and before the end of her extended probationary period, began a grievance procedure against him. She is now working under a different manager, and, after a series of training sessions on organizational skills, she has been commended for being the most highly organized person in the team. The grievance case has been quietly dropped.

In another case, a PA reported to two managers who had very different styles of management. The first manager organized the tasks the PA needed to do in advance and forwarded instructions about them to her by e-mail. Then the PA was able to carry out these tasks calmly and efficiently. The second manager, by contrast, often walked into the office demanding information on the spot. This left the PA frozen with anxiety and unable to retrieve any information efficiently from her mind, or from her files. Yet all that was needed here was for the second manager to understand how to help his PA work more effectively – once this had been achieved, tensions on both sides dissolved.

As we have seen in Robert's case, once there is awareness and understanding of 'hidden' disabilities, it is often small adjustments in the way that tasks are managed that can make a significant difference to a person's work performance.

Conclusion

Disputes around dyslexia often emerge when there are changes at work which tend to uncover or highlight an employee's difficulties. The changes could come about through promotion to a new position, the appointment of a new line manager, the loss of a supportive colleague, or changes in the workplace environment. In such cases, an individual who was previously coping well with his work may now find himself in need of extra support. And the individual's line manager and colleagues also need to understand the nature of his difficulties, so that they can take proper account of them.

Awareness of hidden disabilities, however, needs to spread more widely than this. Inclusive workplaces are those where there is a whole-organization understanding that adjustments may be needed to support people with particular difficulties to allow them to make full use of their particular skills and talents.

I might go further. If, in the organizational culture, there was an embedded understanding of difference, and acceptance of adjustments as the norm, *all* employees might be enabled to utilize their strengths and to work to the best of their abilities. The benefits are great: individuals are likely to be more confident and effective, and the organization is likely to be more productive and successful. Discrimination against those with difficulties or different working styles will belong to the past. It is then that disputes around dyslexia and other hidden disabilities will drop away.

INFORMATION POINT F

Access to Work Disability Support

Katherine Kindersley

The Access to Work (AtW) programme is a government scheme run by JobcentrePlus which provides support for disabled people and their employers. It offers information and advice as well as financial assistance towards the extra costs of employing a person with a disability. It is available to employed and self-employed people as well as to unemployed people who are applying for jobs. It covers any type of job: full-time or part-time, permanent or temporary.

The definition of disability as given in the Disability Discrimination Act of 1995 (DDA) is 'a *physical or mental impairment* which has a *substantial* and *long-term adverse effect* on a person's ability to carry out *normal day-to-day activities*' (see Information point H). People with dyslexia, dyspraxia, or other learning difficulties of a specific or general nature may therefore be eligible to apply for AtW support.

The employee may need to provide evidence of his/her dyslexia or other specific learning difficulties in the form of a full diagnostic assessment report. AtW will not pay for this diagnostic assessment, but the employer may be willing to do so. The employee then needs to arrange a Workplace Needs assessment, either through AtW, or through a private dyslexia organization which specializes in workplace consultancy. In either case, the resulting report can be used to apply for AtW grants for equipment and training.

If AtW is to carry out the assessment, it is the individual and not the employer who must make the initial application. Once AtW has agreed the recommendations made in the Workplace Needs assessment, they

Dyslexia and Employment Edited by Sylvia Moody
© 2009 John Wiley & Sons, Ltd

will write to the employee and the employer. The employer would then purchase the equipment and commission the necessary training, and claim the agreed amount back from AtW.

The Workplace Needs assessment will determine the employee's needs, taking into account information from the employee's diagnostic report and the particular demands of his/her job, and will also make detailed recommendations for support. The recommendations could include some or all of the following:

- Assistive technology.
- Specialist IT training.
- A detailed workplace skills training programme, to be carried out by a specialist in adult dyslexia.
- Adjustments the employer can make in workplace practice to support the employee.

When a recommendation is made for workplace skills training, AtW requires the amount of training time suggested to be broken down into detailed areas and to be explicitly related to overcoming specific problems arising out of the job. For example:

> *Time management – 5 hours.* To overcome the employee's problems with time management and with organising and prioritising work tasks.
> *Writing skills – 10 hours.* To help overcome problems with written language skills, such as spelling, grammar, appropriate language use, organising ideas, creating formal report structures.

AtW will require a follow-up report detailing how the training has helped the individual to become more efficient in his/her work.

Some Workplace Needs assessments may focus on equipment support and fail to make provision for individual skills training by a specialist. However, this skills training can often form the most valuable part of the support package for a person with dyslexia. If, therefore, such training is not recommended in the assessment report, the employee should ask AtW to fund a supplementary assessment with an adult dyslexia specialist who can devise and carry out such a programme.

The employer should be made aware that workplace skills training for people with dyslexia is more successful if it is spread over a period of months, as this allows time for new skills to be practised and improvement to be monitored.

People with dyslexia will not always be 'disabled' in the strict legal sense, but employers may still be willing to give them support by commissioning a Workplace Needs assessment and implementing its recommendations.

Funding

At the time of writing, AtW will pay

- 100% of approved costs in the case of unemployed people who have gained work and who have a confirmed start date, self-employed people, and people who have been employed for less than 6 weeks;
- 100% of approved costs of people changing jobs.

For employed people who have been with their employer for 6 weeks or longer, AtW will not make any contribution to costs below £300. Above this figure, AtW will pay up to 80% of the costs up to £10 000, with the employer paying 20%; and up to 100% of the costs above £10 000.

AtW will also pay up to 100% of all approved costs, irrespective of the type of employment, for the following:

- Travel to work.
- Communicator support at interview.
- A support worker if someone needs practical help because of their disability, either at work or in getting to work.

AtW funding is made available for up to 3 years. If further funding is requested after this time, the applicant's circumstances and support needs will need to be reviewed. AtW funding is not available retrospectively and it will not refund any payments that have already been made towards the cost of reasonable adjustments.

The total time from application to reimbursement of costs of equipment should be within 40 working days, although applications for assistance with interviews can be processed more quickly.

AtW support may result in a business benefit, for example, if other members of staff use the specialist equipment as part of their own work. In these cases, the business benefit costs will be estimated and deducted from the AtW grant.

The AtW programme is administered by JobcentrePlus.

Visit: jobcentreplus.gov.uk and search for 'Access to Work'.

CHAPTER 8

A Dyslexic Employee Speaks

Jeffrey Till

This is a transcript of a conversation between Jeffrey Till, a dyslexic engineer in a large telecommunications organization, Katherine Kindersley, director of Dyslexia Assessment and Consultancy, and Sylvia Moody, the editor of this book.

SM: Thank you, Jeffrey, for coming to talk to us today about your experiences as a dyslexic person in the workplace. The first thing I'd like to ask you is: Am I correct in thinking that, although you've been with your present company for a good many years, it's only quite recently that you disclosed your dyslexia to your employers?

JT: That's right, it was only about 2 years ago, though I had realized myself that I was dyslexic about 7 years before that.

SM: And so I suppose that means your life could be divided into two phases – Jeffrey before disclosure and Jeffrey after disclosure – you might say Jeffrey BD and Jeffrey AD. So perhaps we could start with the Jeff BD – can you give us an idea of your general background – how you managed at school?

JT: I didn't. My exam results were always appalling, but that seemed to be in line with the expectations of my teachers. My own expectations of myself were very different, though – I was always thinking: I can do better than this. This isn't acceptable.

KK: So how did you yourself feel about this situation at the time – were you frustrated? Depressed?

Dyslexia and Employment Edited by Sylvia Moody
© 2009 John Wiley & Sons, Ltd

JT: Frustration was the biggest thing – having to work three times as hard as everyone else to achieve not even half of what they did. I always thought I had more in me than what could come out on paper.

KK: What happened when you left school?

JT: Well, first I worked in a warehouse – just an unskilled job, and obviously that wasn't very satisfying for me.

SM: And how did you move on from there?

JT: Well, my expectations of myself always made me look around for something better. I saw an advert for my present company encouraging people to apply to train as engineers, and I applied for that.

KK: So you did your training on the job?

JT: Yes. I went in as an adult recruit and attended classes in the evening.

SM: Did your course tutors pick up on your dyslexia?

JT: Not really – the only person who ever did was a teacher I once had at school – she said she thought I might be dyslexic, but this was never followed up. At the time that I applied for my present job, I would not have thought of describing myself as dyslexic.

SM: So that meant you couldn't really talk to people about your difficulties with or without the label?

JT: Absolutely. It was all the years of people thinking that I was thick – being put in the lowest classes at school and no one having any faith in me.

KK: And what about your job – were your difficulties evident to your colleagues?

JT: No, I managed to hide it all very well at work – at least during the years when everything was more or less automated and you could get away with things fairly easily. I think my problem was more my insecurity about myself – not really knowing what I was capable of.

SM: And did you see that situation just going on forever? Did you see any way out of it at all?

JT: I think I just assumed it *would* go on forever. I'd got used to getting other people to do things for me if I couldn't do them, and with technology coming in, that helped a lot from the point of view of spellcheckers and so on.

SM: So how did it come about that you moved on from Jeff BD – the before disclosure phase? What brought about the change?

JT: I suppose I got to a point where the job was getting more complicated – there was more written work – and it got difficult for me to cope with it. I suppose in some sort of desperation I went back to the word that that teacher had used all those years ago – dyslexia – and sort of clung on to it. I'd never been really sure what it meant, but I heard one or two people talking about it, and I starting thinking 'am I or aren't I'?

KK: So you decided to check it out?

JT: Yes, I went onto the British Dyslexia Association web site and did a self-check – and that seemed to say I was dyslexic.

SM: So did that prompt you to approach your employer about it?

JT: No, it was 7 years before I said anything to my employer.

SM: Seven years of working up to it?

JT: Yes.

KK: So did something particular happen that decided you in the end to tell your employer? Was there a particular event that tipped you over?

JT: Yes – I think there were two points – one was reaching 40, a mid-life crisis possibly! – but the other thing was that I got elected onto the CWU National Executive and found myself swamped by a whole lot of paperwork and administration. From the intelligence point of view I could manage the work, but the issue obviously was my lack of reading and writing – it stopped me achieving what I wanted to achieve. So at that point I thought: I've got a choice – I can walk away or I can actually confront this, and that's when I told my employers.

SM: And how did they react?

JT: Brilliantly – they arranged for me to have a full assessment, and said they would be happy to support me in every way possible.

SM: And how was the actual experience of the assessment? I imagine you were nervous having spent so many years trying to gather together the courage to do it?

JT: The assessment in one way was the most difficult thing I've done in my life – I didn't enjoy the experience – but at the same time I would say it was the best thing I've done in my life.

SM: Was the psychologist who assessed you able to explain all your strengths and difficulties to you properly?

JT: Yes, he made everything very clear and he was quite encouraging about me pursuing all my ambitions. He said things would be a lot easier with proper support.

SM: Were you also able to talk about your emotions – the years of frustration and your anxiety about the assessment itself?

JT: Yes, I just poured everything out, and the main thing I felt at the end of it was the most massive relief. That's the main feeling I remember now – this huge relief that everything was explained and out in the open.

KK: And what happened as a result of the assessment? How did you move on from there?

JT: Well, my employers paid for some training from a dyslexia specialist. It was the training that made all the difference really. It was more than just about getting skills – it was getting confidence, seeing that I could manage things I wouldn't have imagined doing before.

KK: Did you get IT support as well?

JT: Yes – they gave me text-to-speech software so I could actually listen to documents, and the Dragon programme so I could dictate documents myself to the computer. This opened a lot of doors for me.

KK: So now at work, Jeff, have things also changed as regards the way you relate to other people?

JT: Yes, I don't have to keep on trying to hide my dyslexia – in fact I take every opportunity now to remind people about it! Dyslexia obviously is not something they can see and they tend to keep forgetting.

SM: So you feel more confident about asking your colleagues for help?

JT: Yes, for example, I am always reminding them to use coloured paper because taking the glare off paper helps me a lot, and I'm better at asking people to write things down for me rather than trying to struggle to write them myself. So far I haven't come across anybody – not to my face anyway – who has had a problem with this, so it's been a positive experience from that point of view.

KK: And what about meetings? Are you able to contribute to meetings as well as you would like?

JT: Well, to be honest, I am still a bit scared of speaking out at meetings because I still don't feel completely confident about that. There's all the years of thinking that I was 'thick' and didn't have anything important to say. Sometimes when I'm saying something at a meeting, I suddenly think: you can't be doing this, Jeffrey Till, you shouldn't be taking up space like this.

KK: But at least you've gained the confidence to talk openly to people in less formal settings?

JT: Yes definitely. I might feel a bit awkward sometimes, but I'm not ashamed in the way I was before – and that is a very big thing.

KK: So one of the most valuable things that has come out of the whole process of you going through an assessment is that you are a more confident person generally?

JT: Yes – it's amazing – once you understand what your difficulties are, your attitude and your coping mechanisms change totally.

SM: This whole question of confidence and self-esteem: I suppose it's a bit difficult to change from being ashamed to being completely confident overnight. From what you say it sounds as if you feel in a bit of a mix at the moment – in one way you've got a newfound confidence but in another way you seem to be saying you can still feel somehow unworthy to be in the position you are.

JT: Definitely. The confidence is there and it's growing but that's only been happening for a couple of years. You've got to set that against over 30 years of it not being there. And I'm still very aware of my inability to write things down in the way I want – yes, I can talk the talk, but I can't put it down in writing in a good way, and that can still make me feel inadequate.

SM: It's strange really if you think about it – the fact that a person can't read and write – which a lot of people in many societies can't do just because they haven't had the advantage of an education – that shouldn't really colour one's image of oneself as a person. After all, reading and writing are learnt skills and they don't have much to do with the essential qualities that you have as a person. It's almost as if, in the past at least, you were defining yourself by your difficulties.

JT: Yes, I think that people like me, people of my age, have tended to do that because, when we were young, there was no awareness about dyslexia – whereas today people grow up feeling quite positive about it. But if you don't get that encouragement when you're young, you just become a person who can't read and write. That's you – it's the centre of everything.

SM: So it seems that now you are realizing that you are so much more than a person who can't read and write, that you have many qualities to offer – you are more aware of what is the essential you?

JT: Well, yes, I've really only just started the process of finding out who I essentially am!

KK: From the work you are doing now, it seems obvious that you are in fact a good communicator. You are doing a lot in your work on the National Executive to spread the word about dyslexia and encourage people to follow your example and disclose their difficulties.

JT: I think this is something that is very important for me – I really feel very strongly that I don't want other people to go through what I went through for so many years. I want to tell them – look, I found my way out of this – you can too, but you have to be up front about your problems.

KK: Would you recommend that a person was up front about their problems when they were applying for a job?

JT: Well, if you asked me now, I would say yes. But if you had asked me before I went through the process of assessment and disclosure, I would have said no. It's a very scary thing and you have to be very brave to do it, if you don't have somebody supporting you. It would be difficult to talk about dyslexia to an interview panel if you didn't really understand your difficulties or know what help you needed.

KK: From the experience of your work now on the National Executive, do you think that employers are now much more aware of dyslexia than they used to be?

JT: I think the situation is patchy. It can all come down to a particular line manager – if they know something about dyslexia, or are prepared to learn about it.

SM: What about the Human Resources people – would they not know about dyslexia these days?

JT: Personally I went through my line manager, and I didn't really have contact with HR. In general though, to be honest, I don't think HR people are very clued up about dyslexia – and this is one of the things I'm trying to get changed. I think they often refer people to the Occupational Health department as if dyslexia is some sort of illness or something.

SM: Do you think that your efforts are succeeding at least to some extent in making management generally more informed about dyslexia?

JT: It's definitely more on the agenda now than it has been in the past. So that's a positive step. We've recently produced a work sheet for employers telling them about dyslexia, how to handle it, and where to go for more information.

KK: And, apart from the fact sheet, have you taken any more initiatives?

JT: Yes, in my organization we have a discussion forum which is open for everybody in the company to come to. One particularly useful thing about this is that people who are actually working for the company at all different levels come forward in the forum and say that they are dyslexic – even some quite senior managers. This is a lot better than pointing to famous people like Richard Branson and saying, look, he's got dyslexia – we can't all be Richard Bransons – we need to have ordinary people as our models.

SM: One thing that occurs to me is that there are obviously going to be quite a few managers, possibly senior ones, in the company who are themselves dyslexic and who may never have disclosed it. They may be relying heavily on an assistant or technology to get them through. So I wonder if it might be difficult for such a manager if one of their employees – somebody in a relatively 'humble' position – comes forward in an assertive way and says 'Hey, I'm dyslexic. I want help. I've got rights.' I suppose the manager might secretly envy them.

JT: Yes, I've had managers coming through in their 50s, coming out of the closet and saying: is it too late for me now? – and I'm able to encourage them to have a proper assessment and get more support. They see younger people coming forward boldly to say they're dyslexic and they think 'Well, why shouldn't I?'

SM: I recently interviewed a former Human Resources manager [see Chapter 2] who is now a dyslexia specialist. He made the point that it is vital that good practice on dyslexia is embedded in an organization's policy and processes at every stage – recruitment, appraisal, training, and so on. Can I take it you would agree with that?

JT: One hundred percent. That is at the heart of what I am trying to do with my work – to get companies to embed this policy, not have it as an add-on. In particular it's important to have policies in place that make it easier for people to disclose their dyslexia – whether this is through having some form of disclosure document or having mentors, like myself, in the company who people could speak to in confidence about their concerns. I want it to be easy for people to take the step I took with so much difficulty. I don't want them to go through the 7 years of misery that I went through.

SM: Well, throughout our talk today you have certainly come across as a person who is now positive about your situation. You seem energized, purposeful – certainly no longer skulking in a cupboard.

JT: I've no time for skulking – there's too much to do.

SM: I would imagine that it must be a satisfaction to you now to be in a position when you can use so many of the strengths that you have – intelligence, creativity, communication skills, and so on. Does it feel quite exciting to find yourself putting all these talents to good use, fulfilling yourself and helping other people at the same time?

JT: Yes, it's sort of satisfying and scary at the same time. It's as if I'm discovering things about myself every day and I'm always wondering – and sometimes worrying – about what I'll discover next!

SM: Well, it seems to have been good news so far! Jeff – I'd like to thank you very much for allowing us to share your experiences in your voyage of discovery. I know we would both like to congratulate you on everything you've achieved – I'm sure many people will be able to relate to what you've been saying, and, with luck, they may be inspired to follow your example and find a way, as you did, to come out of the cupboard and take on the world. Thank you for your time.

CHAPTER 9

How to Set Up a Workplace Skills Training Programme

In this chapter, I shall be looking at ways in which a skills training programme can be designed to meet the needs of dyslexic people in a variety of jobs and professions. In the first half of the chapter, I shall concentrate on general skills, such as organizational, memory, and literacy skills, which are required in most jobs. In the second half of the chapter, I shall look at particular cases – drawn mainly from the world of the creative arts and technology – in which the trainer had to be innovative in finding solutions to her client's problems. (In this chapter, feminine pronouns refer to the trainer, masculine pronouns to the client.)

A workplace skills training programme is usually complemented by an IT training programme. For information on the latter see Chapter 6.

Assessment Reports

The employee will have had a diagnostic assessment identifying his specific learning difficulties, and a Workplace Needs assessment (WNA) identifying his work difficulties and training needs. The recommendations made in the WNA report will be based on careful consideration of the information contained in the diagnostic report, the employee's general job description, the particular tasks involved in his job, and the views of both employer and employee on the latter's strengths and difficulties. The report will give the employer detailed information about a suitable training programme, the length of time this training

Dyslexia and Employment Edited by Sylvia Moody
© 2009 John Wiley & Sons, Ltd

is likely to take, and recommendations for organizations or individuals who could carry out the training.

It is vitally important that the training is done by a person who has the qualifications, skills, and experience to work with adults in employment rather than in education. It should also be noted that the training needs of dyslexic adults are *not* usually met by short intensive training courses or general adult literacy classes. Rather, the specialist training needs to be spread out over a period of months to allow time for skills to be practised, different strategies to be tried out, and, if necessary, emotional issues to be properly addressed.

What Does the Training Cover?

A comprehensive training programme could cover any or all of the following:

- Organizational skills.
- Memory strategies.
- Literacy skills (basic or high-level, as required).
- Note-taking techniques.
- Speaking and listening skills.
- Accuracy in number work/data entry.
- Dealing with distressing emotions.
- Interacting positively with managers/colleagues.

These areas cannot be dealt with all at once. The skilled trainer will know how to separate out the various strands and to make appropriate decisions about where to begin and how to tailor the programme to a particular individual in a particular job. She will base the training on real work tasks and real job requirements, weaving in and out of the different areas of need and building up skills in a structured and complementary way. She will progress from the more basic skills training to the higher level skill areas at the appropriate time, and will ensure that new skills are consolidated through regular reviews and reminders. The ultimate purpose of the training is to enable the employee to work independently, using the skills and strategies he has learned in a confident and flexible manner in both his current and any future work situation.

The employer can also expect the trainer to

- give *general* advice on IT and electronic/technological aids;
- carry out part of the training on computer, if required;
- advise both employer and employee on sources of funding for training;
- advise both employer and employee on legal rights and obligations;
- liaise closely with line managers and HR managers to discuss their ongoing concerns, and advise on further adjustments as needed;
- provide awareness training for managers, if requested.

A More Detailed Look at a Training Programme

At the beginning of a training programme, the trainer may well focus on organizational and memory skills, as difficulties in these areas are particularly detrimental to work efficiency. It is in these areas, too, that progress can often be made relatively quickly – and this results in an employee not only becoming better organized but also feeling more positive and confident about himself.

Organizational skills

The trainer will show the employee how to plan a work schedule. One way to do this is for the employee first to set up a timetable for routine tasks. He can write down, in separate lists, all the tasks he needs to do on a daily basis (e.g. answer e-mails), on a weekly basis (e.g. filing), and on a monthly basis (e.g. order stationery). Once the tasks are written down, they become more manageable because they can be assigned regular time slots in the working day. This means that routine work does not build up 'unnoticed'.

The employee also needs to learn an efficient method for prioritizing activities. He may like to have filing trays in different colours – red for 'do this now', green for 'this week', brown for 'pending', and so on, and he can enter these tasks on his timetable in the appropriate colours.

Many tasks are too large to be tackled in just one day, but such large projects are usually known about well in advance. A good approach is to plan backwards. First, the employee writes the deadline into his timetable. He then divides the project into sections, estimating how long each of these sections will take to plan, prepare, and complete. He then draws a flow chart showing the dates on which he must start each section. Dyslexic employees are often surprised to see how early the first section must be begun.

With good forward planning in place, it becomes easier to manage a project, whether this be a written report, a funding application, or the research and planning for a new group training programme. In many large tasks, information must be gathered from other people. If this arrives '*en masse*' there is a danger that the employee will feel overwhelmed. However, if he can work out in advance what is needed, and how the information could be best structured for his purposes, he can then give relevant guidance to those providing the information. His task will then become less demanding because the sifting, organizing, and structuring of information will have already been done.

The best methods for organization are simple, practical, and easy to follow and maintain. Manageable 'To do' lists, an efficient diary, effective filing systems, colour-coded files, clearly labelled storage areas, planners, telephone alarms, electronic organizers, mind maps – all these can provide effective support.

A trainer may teach the 'mind-mapping' technique for organizing ideas, planning activity, and recording information quickly. Once ideas are written down on paper or on screen, it is easier to group them together in different sections and order the sections into a logical sequence. The technique can be used in a wide range of activities: writing, preparing talks, or supporting memory, for example, in a learning or revision process. It is also useful in decision making, and for prioritizing work, as it allows all pending work tasks to be simultaneously seen and considered, without the need for holding them in memory. A number of computer programs offer a mind-mapping facility.

It is important for the trainer to work closely with managers in supporting the individual employee. For example, a manager could ensure that the employee was putting into practice the strategies he had been taught. He/she could also give help with

- planning routine daily schedules;
- setting regular checkpoints during the day;
- drawing up action lists;
- prioritizing tasks into urgent/soon/long term;
- allowing time for planning before tasks;
- devising effective systems for filing, storing, and linking information.

Memory

The second area where dyslexic difficulties are likely to have a general impact on workplace efficiency is that of short-term or 'working' memory. Short-term memory is the memory we use to store information in our minds for a brief time (e.g. a telephone number). If we want to use stored information in some way (e.g. do a sum in our head), then our short-term memory becomes a 'working memory'.

Memory skills are important in 'multi-processing' activities, such as reading comprehension, drafting written documents, keeping track of ideas in a discussion, and expressing oneself logically and succinctly in speech. If information is well organized in the ways suggested in the previous section, it is easier for the mind to hold onto and recall it. The trainer will also show the employee specific strategies for supporting memory. These are likely to include

- recording information in a systematic way;
- recording information in an alternative format, for example, using a digital recorder;
- developing a routine which follows a planned sequence;
- devising strategies for dealing with interruptions;
- displaying visual reminders/visual displays/colour codes;
- requesting clarification of instructions or written backup;
- requesting written backup for telephone conversations and meetings;
- developing strategies for recalling the content of written material;
- developing attention, concentration, and listening skills.

Once an employee has memory strategies such as these in place, he can become resourceful in developing his own strategies to manage particular difficulties. One employee working in an open-plan office was often interrupted in mid-task by his manager asking him to turn his attention to some other pressing matter – and as a result he would forget where he was in his own task. Later, when he returned to his task, he had to think it through all over again – a source of much frustration to him.

His solution was to keep a store of bright yellow paper on his desk with the words 'NEXT STEP' photocopied across the top of each sheet. If interrupted in his work, he would quickly write down the next step in his current task on one of the yellow sheets. When he returned, his note took him straight back to where he was in his task. This simple, effective strategy has enabled him to work more efficiently without wasting time. His line manager now also understands that he is more productive if there are agreed times that he can work without interruptions.

Literacy skills

Almost all jobs require literacy skills and many people report that their job involves more reading and writing now than previously. The trainer will focus the training on the particular literacy needs of an employee in his particular job.

(a) Reading

It may be necessary to begin by teaching basic skills such as reading quickly and accurately. Or the training may concentrate on higher level skills, such as how to identify important information in a text, and how to absorb and hold onto this information. The trainer will work with the employee's own work documents whenever possible.

Examples of strategies which may be used to improve reading skills are:

- Improving underlying word and letter decoding.
- Analyzing the structure of a text before concentrating on content.
- Reviewing, underlining, highlighting, visualization.
- Constructing spider charts or mind maps to 'anchor' or secure content in the mind.
- Becoming an 'active' reader engaged with the text.
- Skimming and scanning text.
- Using lines, colours, spaces, headings, bold print, capitals, patterns, or flow charts to break up the text into manageable sections.

(b) Writing and notetaking

Writing tasks are ubiquitous in the workplace. Most employees have to be able to compose e-mails or letters, and they may have to keep written records of their activities and their progress with various projects. People in managerial or professional jobs often have to write lengthy reports or information documents.

The writing process is a complex one and difficulties can become manifest in a variety of ways. The trainer will be experienced in teaching techniques for spelling, brainstorming for ideas, grouping ideas in a logical way, and structuring material at both sentence and text level.

The employee may need to take notes in various situations, for example in 'live' meetings, or from audio recordings or books. Meeting notes may be an informal record for the employee himself, or they may be formal Minutes for distribution to all participants in the meeting. The trainer will be able to advise on techniques for taking notes in all these situations.

Speaking and listening skills

There are many situations in a working day which make demands on speaking and listening skills. Dyslexic employees often report difficulties in the following areas:

- Pronouncing words.
- Stuttering or stumbling if under pressure, or put on 'the spot'.
- Retrieving the right words, or remembering what to say.
- Presenting thoughts clearly and succinctly.
- Contributing to meetings/discussions.
- Dealing with interviews and work reviews.
- Making presentations or delivering training courses.
- Following verbal instructions.
- Following key points in conversations/discussions.

The trainer could suggest a number of techniques:

- Strategies for focusing and maintaining attention.
- Preparation and planning, for example, making mind maps of the main points in a talk in advance.
- Rehearsal, modelling the role, and role-plays.
- Working on tone and volume of voice and pace of delivery.
- Practising the feeling of confident stance and eye contact.
- Observing and interpreting others' body language.
- Ways of taking control, for example
  - asking others to speak more slowly or to repeat/re-phrase something;
  - talking through thought processes aloud;

- using 'fill-in' phrases to allow thinking time;
- developing the confidence to correct oneself, perhaps by re-phrasing something more appropriately or accurately.

Number work

Many jobs involve working with numbers – for example, copying or making data entries, analyzing graphs or tables of figures, dealing with budgets and financial forecasts, doing numerical calculations, reporting quarterly figures or trading prices. The trainer can help the employee find ways to work more accurately and efficiently by teaching the following methods:

- Splitting and chunking numbers.
- Ways of checking and proofreading.
- Colour-coding segments of tables containing numbers.
- Using visual techniques to learn basic mathematical processes.
- Systematic scanning of graphs/charts/tables of data.

Emotions and interaction with colleagues

Many people who have dyslexia or other forms of specific learning difficulty report a variety of distressing emotions, ranging from anxiety, embarrassment, frustration and low self-esteem to panic, stress, depression, and despair. These may interfere in a significant way with performance and career development. (See Chapter 10 for a more detailed discussion of this topic.)

The trainer will be able to help the employee manage their emotions more effectively by drawing on a variety of techniques, for example

- visualization;
- relaxation;
- rehearsing situations in advance;
- monitoring and moderating defensive/aggressive behaviour.

The tutor will also encourage the employee to be more assertive and will bolster his confidence by helping him to recognize his strengths and talents. She will also suggest ways in which he could interact more successfully with his colleagues. Finally, the trainer will be able to provide advice on

- the emotional effects of dyslexia;
- disclosure issues;
- ways of maintaining psychological well-being, for example, taking regular exercise/attending yoga classes/practising meditation. (For a more detailed discussion on disclosure, see Information point C.)

Different Workplaces

The world of employment is tremendously varied and there is no such thing as a standard training programme. While most working people will benefit from having good organizational, memory, and literacy skills, every job will make its own demands. The nature of each problem needs to be clearly defined if the appropriate solution is to be found. A trainer, therefore, must be flexible, resourceful, and innovative. Below are some examples of workplace problems – drawn mainly from the world of the creative arts and technology – which required idiosyncratic solutions.

Specialized Computer Work

Specialist computer programmes, used across a wide range of employment sectors, can place heavy demands on working memory, typically an area of weakness for the person with dyslexia. Below are two examples taken respectively from the world of computer programming and the world of film animation.

Problem 1

An IT engineer had to work on database corruptions, managing and resolving service requests logged by customers in respect of his company's computer products. The complex codes and 'trace' files were held in numerous files, layered one behind the other on his computer. Compared with his colleagues he worked very slowly because he could not hold all the relevant information in memory at the same time and had to keep going back to check the various screens.

Problem 2

A film animator had to work simultaneously with a number of screens as he edited images and synchronized them with the soundtrack. He found it difficult to work at complex levels with one monitor because he could not recall or coordinate different elements from the layers of screens which were not in view. As a result his work was also slow.

Solution

These problems with short-term memory and coordination of information in two very different settings were resolved in a similar way. Additional monitors were added enabling more information to be simultaneously displayed. The engineer could then analyze trace files more effectively. The animator could see the sound files at the same time as the images, and this enabled him to synchronize one with the other with the split-second timing that is essential in animation.

Design

Many dyslexic designers working across a range of design areas have an ability to solve design briefs in an organic, intuitive way, often by working directly with their materials. Yet, because they just 'arrive' at the solution, using instinct rather than logic, they often have difficulty explaining the rationale behind their solution to other people. This causes problems when they are working collaboratively within a design team.

Problem

A fashion designer struggled to move between two- and three-dimensional forms during the design process. In particular, she had problems translating her creative ideas into the 'flat' two-dimensional sketches used by the team in their discussions before the sketches were refined into cutting patterns. She needed to work with her materials in a concrete way, manipulating the fabrics directly on the model. In her compositions, contrasts between materials of different weights played an important role; she would experiment, for example with placing heavy masculine metals against chiffon and feminine fabrics. She needed to have a method of recording the different ideas and the effect of the different placement of materials, so that they could be compared, contrasted, and discussed with the design team.

Solution

A digital camera enabled her to 'capture' the different compositions she had used and transfer the camera images straight to her computer, where they could be manipulated as needed. Through being able to capture the images in this way, she was able to demonstrate her thought processes and the reasons for her design solutions to the rest of the team, and so work more effectively with colleagues.

Textile Construction

Problem

A trainee colour technician in a textile construction company had difficulty in making up the dye mixes. The need for accuracy was crucial but she found it hard to

- remember the precise quantity of ingredients needed for each dye;
- follow the correct sequence of actions in making up the dye mixes;
- calculate the different proportions of ingredients for different volumes of dye.

Solution

For each dye recipe, the technician was helped to produce

(i) an audio recording of the instructions which could be reviewed as needed.
(ii) a colour-coded flow chart showing the ingredients and quantities which had to be added at each stage of the process.

Music

Problem 1: visual difficulties

Musicians with dyslexia (or dyspraxia) often report visual processing problems. Scores can look 'confusing' and the lines of the staves and the notes appear to shift about on the page, making reading of the notation difficult.

Solution

Some musicians prefer to play without music, and to rely instead on memory, especially in public performances. Sometimes music can be enlarged, and colour can also be used to separate and structure sections of the score. One musician who had severe visual processing problems used to cut out her lines from the orchestral score and paste them onto grey paper, allowing plenty of space around each line so that she could process the notes more easily.

Problem 2: synchronization

Sight-reading scores can be difficult, as this involves reading a written symbolic code and synchronizing the notes with the sequence of movements needed to play an instrument, or with the breathing and production of voice sounds in singing. Difficulties with sight-reading can make auditions or rehearsals extremely stressful.

Solution

Techniques to develop skills in sight-reading scores might include the following:

- Paying particular attention to the structure of the score.
- Focussing on the first beat in each bar and holding onto that 'at all costs'.
- Looking out for patterns and repetitions.

- Fingering through sections of a piece (e.g. on the knee) to rehearse a sequence before playing and to provide a 'muscle memory' for the fingers.
- Transposing a sequence or section into a familiar pattern or song.

Also, rehearsing in a group can develop confidence and encourage an individual to persevere with a difficult piece. The other players act as a sort of metronome, emphasizing the structure and rhythm.

In auditions or examinations, an appropriate concession would be to allow the candidate to look over scores before having to sight-read.

Problem 3: singing in a foreign language

Singers often have to learn songs in a foreign language, and this is a particular challenge for a dyslexic singer. Poor memory will make it hard for him to remember both the words of a song and their correct pronunciation; poor sequencing skills will make it arduous for him to look words up in a dictionary.

Solution

A good solution could be the provision of a personal digital assistant with text to speech technology, and also loaded with a 'talking partner dictionary', a bi-directional translator package of the European languages. This provides a fast and efficient way of translating the words and phrases of foreign language songs: it shows the text in both languages on screen, and this can then be heard/read aloud. This not only helps with pronunciation but also provides a multi-sensory way of learning.

Theatre and Stage Management

Difficulty with reading accurately and efficiently can interfere with an actor's performance at 'blind' auditions, and so with his chances of success. However, as in musical auditions, additional time to look at material in advance is a reasonable adjustment. An actor may also find it difficult to quickly master movements or dance routines, as these need a good sense of rhythm, orientation, and direction. Again, extra time could be given for rehearsal and practice.

Many jobs in the world of theatre involve reading, understanding, marking up, and accurately following scripts. A lighting technician must be able to follow a script while dealing with complex lighting charts, grids, and graphs as well as controlling switches in a lighting panel. Once a play is in progress, there are huge demands on 'multi-processing' skills with many activities 'live' and no opportunity to stop or go back.

Sometimes there can be confusion between 'Stage Left' and 'Stage Right', or with mentally translating two-dimensional set plans into the three-dimensional space of the theatre. This can cause problems for the stage management crew and stage set designers. In all these situations, the trainer will have to work in an imaginative way to help find supportive strategies to alleviate the difficulties.

The strategies will vary according to each particular situation. Examples are as follows:

- Colour coordinating sections of scripts with lighting charts.
- Visual reminders to help with left/right discrimination and orientation difficulties.
- Construction of simple maquettes for set designs to help visual perceptual and visual-spatial problems.

Remembering Codes

A locksmith working in a large company found it difficult to remember the codes for his lock systems. He often had to resort to using his skills to pick his own locks in order to set them again – and this was time consuming and frustrating. With his trainer, he developed a system of recording each new code into a voice recorder. He replayed this as often as needed in order to transfer the codes accurately onto his computer, where he could print out individual codes as needed. He was also able to remember several master codes by repeatedly tapping them into a telephone keypad, so using his kinaesthetic memory.

Mastering Technical Data

An engineer working on a North Sea oil rig was unable to remember and explain the technical detail he had learnt on training courses, and was therefore unable to pass professional examinations. His trainer worked closely with his managers to devise solutions. Practical demonstrations of the technical processes were filmed, bringing alive the diagrams and dense pages of the text in the manual. The engineer was able to watch these video clips on his computer during the long stretches of time he spent on the North Sea oil platforms. Back at the land base, he talked through the processes with his trainer, which helped him find the words he needed to explain his understanding of what he had learnt. Once he was confident of his explanations, they were recorded onto audio tape. The multi-sensory combination of the visual images and the auditory feedback enabled the engineer to learn his material successfully.

Workplaces may vary greatly, but the above examples illustrate that once a particular difficulty is clearly identified, a solution can usually be found.

Liaison with Managers

There needs to be an agreed system for communication between the trainer and the employer, so that the line manager, in particular, can support the training by identifying priority areas, providing feedback on progress, and giving support to the employee. The trainer can also advise managers on adjustments which might be made in workplace practice. (See Information point B for more information on this.)

However, even with good training and support, an individual employee cannot function efficiently at work if awareness of dyslexia is confined only to himself, his trainer, and his line manager. For this reason, it is desirable that a programme of dyslexia awareness training is provided across the whole organization. There needs to be an understanding by management at all levels of how dyslexia can affect every stage of the employment process: recruitment, training, appraisal, promotion, and perhaps eventually, redundancy. (For a detailed discussion of this, see Chapter 2.)

Conclusion

A programme of properly focussed specialist training for an individual employee is likely to make a significant difference to his efficiency, competence, and confidence, and to enable him to make a more valuable contribution in the workplace. Complementing this training, employers and individual managers can play an essential part in creating an inclusive workplace where dyslexic employees can make good use of their skills and strengths. Workplaces where all employees are well supported are happier, more efficient, and more productive.

INFORMATION POINT G

Careers for Dyslexic Adults

Brian Hagan

Is There a 'Right' Career for a Dyslexic Person?

People with dyslexia or other specific learning difficulties often ask whether there are particular careers that would suit them; or, on the other hand, whether there are particular careers that they should avoid at all costs. There is no simple answer to this question.

Each person has to balance a number of factors: what career actually interests them; what the demands of it are likely to be; and whether they feel that, with appropriate support, they will be able to cope reasonably well with those demands.

In practice, people often find themselves in a career 'by accident'. A decision at the age of 16 about what A-levels to do (perhaps influenced by liking for a particular teacher rather than an interest in a particular subject) will determine what subjects are later studied at college, and ultimately what career is pursued. Once in a job a dyslexic person might realize that the work they are doing does not interest them, or they might like their work but find themselves not competent to do it.

It is hard to decide in advance if a job will be rewarding – and manageable. For a dyslexic person, however, there are some obvious minefields. For example, a person who is a very slow reader might think twice about training as a solicitor or barrister, professions in which large amounts of reading need to be done at short notice. If a person is inaccurate with numbers, perhaps book keeping is not for them; and if they have poor visual skills, then air traffic controller is probably a poor choice.

Dyslexia and Employment Edited by Sylvia Moody
© 2009 John Wiley & Sons, Ltd

There are various ways in which a person can ‘try out’ a job. For example, many professional and vocational trainings (e.g. nursing, drama) include practical experience. The government also runs job trialling schemes (see end of article for relevant web sites).

When considering career choices, dyslexic people need to be fully aware of their strengths as well as their difficulties, and, if possible, choose a job in which their strengths can be utilized. A person who has literacy difficulties may well have excellent interpersonal, practical, or IT skills, or perhaps creative skills and artistic ability. They may have an entrepreneurial flair and be well suited to being self-employed (preferably with a literate secretary). Vague generalizations about what dyslexic people can and cannot do (e.g. ‘dyslexic people have good visual skills’) are not helpful; each person needs to make a careful appraisal of his/her own strengths and weaknesses.

Obtaining Career Advice

In general, career advice for dyslexic adults is sought by three groups of people:

1. Dyslexic adults who are seeking advice on choosing a career which will capitalize on their strengths and motivation, and avoid areas of weakness.
2. Employees who face redundancy or dismissal, or are about to voluntarily leave a job because of performance problems attributable to dyslexia.
3. Employers who want advice on re-deploying a dyslexic employee who cannot cope with his/her present job.

Not all careers advice is customized for dyslexic people. However, a dyslexia-aware careers adviser should work systematically through the following stages:

1. Appraisal

- Consideration of the individual’s general strengths and difficulties, based on self-report and, if available, diagnostic assessment and/or workplace needs reports.
- Consideration of the individual’s professional competencies.

2. Overview of labour market and training opportunities

- Review of various occupations and their characteristics/requirements.
- Advice on reasonable adjustments and training.
- Advice on achieving control at work and in study.

3. Generating options

- Identifying the individual's *niche*, that is, the occupational areas that motivate him/her most.
- Generating options by matching niches to occupational requirements.
- Prioritizing options.
- Drawing up an action plan to select appropriate employment or training.

4. Putting the plan into action

- Explaining how to find dyslexia-friendly employers and get further information on specific careers.
- Setting objectives, for example, making four requests each week for job descriptions and person specifications.
- Setting timescales.
- Providing information to support job applications, including preparing an effective CV, discussing issues of disclosure, and practising interview techniques.
- Suggesting resources relevant to the plan, for example, careers web sites, government support, and helpful publications.

Some Successful Career Changes

Below are three examples of dyslexic people who were unhappy in their job but who, after taking advice from a *dyslexia-aware* careers adviser, made a successful career change.

Jim was very keen to train as a fireman, but during his training, questions arose as to whether his dyslexic difficulties, in particular his slow reaction times, made him unsuitable for this career. His colleagues felt they could not entirely rely on him in an emergency, and as a result he was subject to a fair amount of bullying. Jim eventually gave up the training course, broken hearted that he would not be able to pursue his long-held ambition to join the fire service.

Solution: After discussing his situation with a careers adviser, Jim re-trained as a community safety officer. In this role, he was not required to make on-the-spot decisions: he could organize his time and workload in a flexible way. And he had the satisfaction of doing a job he found interesting while offering a useful service to the public.

Beatrice's first job was in customer care at a call centre. Here, she found it impossible to deal with incoming calls within the very strict time limits demanded by the company and became stressed and depressed. Eventually she was dismissed.

Solution: Encouraged by a careers officer to look for a job which utilized her good interpersonal skills, Beatrice trained as a Health Care Assistant and was very successful in this job. It made only limited demands on literacy, did not depend on quick reaction time, and fully utilized her good people skills.

Robert worked as a trainee accountant. Though good with figures, he could not cope with the constant short deadlines and the lack of control over his time and workload. He eventually became depressed and had to leave his job.

Solution: Robert had good IT skills and, on the advice of a careers adviser, he developed these further and set up as a self-employed trainer in assistive technology. He was very successful in this job which drew on his interests, utilized his strengths, and gave him control over work levels and deadlines.

Useful Web Sites

www.direct.gov.uk
www.open.ac.uk/careers
www.learndirect-advice.co.uk
www.prospects.ac.uk

CHAPTER 10

Dyslexia: Attitudes and Emotions

Diana Bartlett

In recent years, employers have become increasingly aware of the varied nature of dyslexic difficulties: they now recognize, therefore, that the term 'dyslexia' denotes not just difficulty with literacy skills but also problems with memory, work organization, time management, and communication. However, their understanding – and sympathy – often stops there: they often remain *unaware* of the range of negative emotions and attitudes that so often accompany dyslexia. And yet these cause as much confusion, and as many problems, in the workplace as the more visible inefficiencies in work performance. Consequently, though employers may be very ready to help dyslexic staff by providing skills training and IT support, they may neglect, or feel unable to deal with, emotional or attitudinal problems. They may in fact regard such problems as best dealt with by disciplinary procedures rather than by making reasonable adjustments.

The emotional effects of dyslexia are particularly marked in people who have not been diagnosed as dyslexic until adulthood. Such people may have spent their lives working twice as hard as others to achieve the same results, only to be judged as lazy when their work does not meet requirements. They may be recognized as intelligent, and so their failure to meet deadlines or to produce work to a satisfactory standard will be seen as 'careless' or 'sloppy'. They may be judged as 'stupid', when in fact they are as intelligent as their colleagues, but just less fluent in communication.

Dyslexia and Employment Edited by Sylvia Moody
© 2009 John Wiley & Sons, Ltd

After years of suffering misunderstandings of this sort, some dyslexic people become aggressive or defensive. Others lose self-esteem and confidence, which further weakens their performance. They may withdraw from their work colleagues and become outsiders. They will almost certainly be frustrated that their dyslexia has prevented them from working at a level commensurate with their actual intelligence and potential. It is little wonder, then, that their emotional state and attitude to work may sometimes, from the employer's point of view, leave something to be desired. They may be seen as rude, uncooperative, even disruptive.

When dyslexic employees first come to me for training, they arrive, more often than not, with a collection of unresolved emotional issues. They may be harbouring feelings of resentment at how they perceive they have been treated at work, and often have a long a list of complaints and grievances. They may be in routine conflict with their managers or work colleagues. They may feel unappreciated and unrewarded at work; or they may feel isolated and misunderstood. They are almost always stressed, anxious, and apprehensive. They will probably not have found a way to talk directly to their managers or colleagues about their difficulties, and usually feel themselves to be at an impasse.

If their dyslexic difficulties include problems with communication – especially oral communication – they will be doubly in need of guidance and support. The dyslexia trainer, therefore, has a twofold task: (a) to give the employee an opportunity to express his feelings and to explore ways in which he might deal with these in a more positive way; and (b) to give guidance to managers on how they can make the workplace feel a less threatening environment for the employee. (Throughout this article, feminine pronouns refer to the trainer, masculine pronouns to the trainee/employee.)

In such a programme it is vital that there is involvement of staff at all levels and in different areas: line managers, work colleagues, human relations personnel, trainers, occupational health personnel, and union representatives. All need to learn how to deal sensitively with the emotions that accompany dyslexia, and so give dyslexic staff a positive experience of the workplace. (See Chapter 2 for an HR manager's perspective on this.)

In this chapter, I will look in detail at the range of negative emotions and attitudes commonly linked with dyslexia. I will consider how these affect relationships in the workplace, and also hinder performance in situations such as interviews, work reviews, training courses, and teamwork. Throughout I will provide illustrative case studies to demonstrate how the dyslexia trainer can work with the employee, managers, and other key staff to resolve conflicts and negotiate solutions acceptable to all parties.

A Detailed Look at Emotions and Attitudes

Anxiety and stress

The most common emotions that dyslexic employees report, and display, are anxiety and stress. These are the almost inevitable result of repeated difficulties in life and at work – of having to suffer routine criticism, misjudgement, and misunderstanding. They have a detrimental effect on work performance because they reduce cognitive efficiency, thereby undermining reasoning ability and impairing clear thought. They can also lead to erratic behaviour – and in extreme cases to panic and confusion – with the result that in the end an employee can feel overwhelmed even by minor tasks.

Together, stress and inefficiency form a vicious circle of continual failure: the more stressed or distressed a person feels about their inefficiency, the more inefficient they will become, and then their distress will again increase.

The dyslexia trainer needs on the one hand to teach the employee effective techniques (e.g. relaxation techniques) for managing his emotional state better, and on the other hand to alert managers to things they might be doing which are making the situation worse. For example, a manager might be in the habit of 'hovering over' an employee when he is working, making frequent critical remarks, but giving little praise.

Fear

Dyslexic difficulties, and the stress associated with them, may lead to fear. This produces a range of avoidance behaviours that can make dyslexic employees appear unmotivated or uncooperative. They may put off doing written or administrative work and thus miss deadlines and generally fall into chaotic work habits. They may be reluctant to ask for help when it is needed, and be deterred from applying for promotion or for training courses. They may often take time off work because of stress or minor ailments.

Managers need to be made aware of the underlying reasons for these apparently uncooperative attitudes. They need to be active in helping the employee to tackle writing or administrative tasks in small manageable stages, and be prepared to relax tight deadlines wherever possible. They could also give encouragement about applying for promotion, and ensure that the employee has extra support when attending training courses.

Low confidence and low self-esteem

Over the years dyslexic people may come to expect that they will perform badly. Routine criticism or dissatisfaction from managers will fill them with increasing self-doubt. This low self-esteem will generalize, and they may become shy and withdrawn, awkward in their behaviour towards their bosses and work colleagues. This may make them appear unfriendly and aloof, and so they will receive little sympathy or support from the people around them.

In my work with such clients I teach them techniques to develop their confidence and become more assertive. These may include basic cognitive psychology techniques to help clients question their negative self-judgements; visualization exercises to help them acknowledge their strengths and to build a more positive self-image; or role-play exercises to practise assertiveness in typical workplace situations.

I also work with managers to advise them on ways in which they could bolster the confidence of an employee. For example, I might suggest that they arrange an assertiveness training course; that they make a point of offering praise where appropriate; or that they ask other staff members to make an effort to be more friendly and understanding towards their dyslexic colleague, and to include him more in workplace conversations and activities.

Defensiveness

Dyslexic people often find themselves 'on the defensive' as a result of all the criticism they have received over the years. This can incline them to blame their failures on others – their managers, their colleagues, or 'the system'. As a result, they can be very hard to work with; they often find themselves in conflict with their bosses or workmates, thus creating disharmony and affecting a department's overall efficiency. In extreme cases, this situation can result in the employee beginning a formal grievance procedure, at which point HR staff and union representatives may become involved in the case. In situations like this I may be called in to mediate between the various interested parties to try to resolve the issue. The following case of a particularly defensive client will illustrate how situations such as this can become very tangled indeed.

Julio came to me for advice about how his workplace difficulties might be tackled. He was extremely stressed and completely convinced that everyone else was to blame for his problems. He felt his bosses 'couldn't be bothered' to support him or understand his dyslexia. He was sure they were trying to get rid of him. He said that his colleagues were hostile and openly expressed resentment about the few concessions he had been given. He had complained about all this to the HR manager who then tried to mediate. But then Julio began to feel that the HR manager was also 'against him'. He had recently contacted his trade union representative to discuss his grievances, but again felt that the representative was not sympathetic to him.

Apart from his habitual defensiveness and blaming of others, one of the reasons that Julio exasperated so many people was his difficulty in putting his concerns into clear words. He tended to overwhelm people with intricate details about his grievances, frequently straying off the point, and severely trying their patience.

After helping Julio to summarize his concerns succinctly in writing – with considerable resistance from him, as he was loathe to leave out any of his detailed complaints – I realized it would probably be better if I, rather than he, tried to explain his defensiveness to the various parties involved. I would be able to put his concerns more briefly than he was able or prepared to do. I therefore had a meeting with all the stakeholders in the case.

Julio's line manager seemed to find it a revelation that Julio's dyslexia might be making him so 'difficult', and began to feel some stirrings of sympathy for him. The HR manager and union representative were greatly relieved to receive a succinct and coherent summary of his problems and grievances, which enabled them to understand his situation better. The HR manager subsequently arranged for me to give a dyslexia awareness talk to Julio's whole department, and this helped his colleagues to understand his negative attitudes. As a result of all this, Julio decided to withdraw his grievance claim, and began to accept that his managers and colleagues might, with proper understanding of his difficulties, be willing to help and support him.

Anger and aggression

Sometimes the negative attitude of a dyslexic employee can go beyond defensiveness and express itself in anger or aggression towards managers and other staff. An aggressive person tends to provoke other people into making aggressive responses, and such a scenario is obviously damaging to office relationships – it can, in fact, disrupt the working of a whole department. An example:

Jeanette came to me full of grievances against her managers. She worked for an employment agency interviewing job seekers and writing summaries of their skills and experience – all difficult tasks for a person with dyslexia. She complained that her managers belittled her and kept her under constant pressure. She said this made her feel angry, and she frequently had outbursts of rage. In one case, she had verbally abused a colleague, and had subsequently been threatened with dismissal if her behaviour did not improve.

In her sessions with me we began work on improving her writing and interviewing skills, but her feelings of wrath towards her bosses remained and tended to dominate our sessions. Although she realized that her attitude was doing her more harm than good, she was still unable to contain her defiant outbursts at work. Again discussions between myself and Jeanette's managers resulted in their adopting a more sympathetic and supportive attitude, and Jeanette also worked with me on learning strategies to control her anger.

We agreed to devote part of each training session to focussing on her anger. We looked at simple techniques, such as taking deep breaths, to help calm her anger. We did role-plays to prepare her for potentially stressful work interactions, so that she could practise dealing with them in a calmer, more coherent manner. I also encouraged her to analyze how she dealt with her anger in particular situations. She began to keep an 'anger diary' in which she wrote how she had succeeded, or failed, to control her anger – and we were able to reflect together on what had gone wrong in the times when she did not succeed.

She and her manager will probably never become friends – but at least they now have a better working relationship, and Jeanette's work performance is beginning to improve.

Frustration

Dyslexic difficulties often prevent people from reaching a level of academic and professional achievement that is commensurate with their intellectual abilities. Naturally this causes them to feel unsatisfied and frustrated, and often simply bored. They lose motivation and appear to be uninterested in doing their job efficiently. This apparent lack of enthusiasm is frustrating to their managers. Although the latter can often see that a dyslexic person is intelligent, they fail to realize that it is precisely this that will make their current, relatively 'lowly', position unsatisfying. They feel let down when the employee appears not to appreciate their attempts to give them help and support.

Here also a dyslexia trainer can help by talking to all parties and encouraging managers to take note of a dyslexic employee's strengths as well as his weaknesses. They may then be willing to consider redeploying the employee to a position which requires more in the way of intelligence and general business acumen than does, say, a clerical job. It is often justly said that dyslexic people make better managers than clerks.

Depression

It will come as no surprise that all the emotional difficulties, communication problems, and conflicts that accompany dyslexia may sometimes cause a person to become depressed. Apart from the personal pain this causes, severe depression can incapacitate a person so much that they feel unable to work. It can, therefore, result in a high rate of absenteeism and long periods of sick leave.

Depressed employees can be very difficult to work with. They are likely to be needy and fiercely focussed on their own misery – and this may become exhausting and draining for their work colleagues. They can pull down the mood of a whole department. The case below illustrates one way in which such problems could be tackled.

Annette was severely dyslexic and, over the years, the burden of her difficulties took such a heavy toll on her that she fell into a severe depression. In our training sessions, she was unable to concentrate on the workplace skills I was trying to teach her, but was obsessed with discussing her depressed state of mind. Presumably the situation was the same in the workplace.

Clearly her depression needed to be tackled before anything else could have a chance of succeeding. I arranged to meet with her manager and suggested that the immediate need was for Annette to have some therapy. I felt that in Annette's case, a brief period of cognitive therapy would not be sufficient, and recommended a more lengthy and intensive type of therapy. As she was unlikely to obtain this through the NHS (National Health Service), and she was unable herself to afford private treatment, I persuaded her manager to approach the HR department to request budget support. We had a joint meeting with the HR manager who eventually agreed to provide funds for a year of weekly therapy. This was the essential starting point to get Annette back on the road to becoming a more positive person and a useful employee.

Over-exuberance

Finally, one 'survival' tactic which some dyslexic people employ is to become, 'over friendly'. It is not uncommon to find a dyslexic employee has become the 'office comedian' in an attempt to hide his inefficiencies and find favour with colleagues and bosses. Although occasionally entertaining, this can become exasperating if carried to an extreme – and it can make the employee appear flippant and unconcerned about improving his work performance. What is usually needed here is for both the trainer and managers to engage in trying to improve the employee's self-confidence, removing his need to use inappropriate, and ultimately counter-productive, means to hide his difficulties and fit into the workplace environment.

Particular Workplace Situations

The range of negative emotions and attitudes described above can extend their tentacles into almost every aspect of a dyslexic employee's job. This section illustrates a few specific workplace situations that can be particularly problematic for dyslexic employees.

Interaction with colleagues

Some dyslexic employees have constant difficulty in interacting well with colleagues. As we have seen, low self-confidence can make them taciturn; defensiveness can make them argumentative; and anger can make them aggressive.

This situation can be made worse if the employee has dyspraxic as well as dyslexic difficulties. Dyspraxic difficulties interfere with both communication and social skills. For example, dyspraxic people may have difficulty in judging the right tone to adopt in a conversation; and they may fail to understand the non-verbal signals which other people give them. They may not express their thoughts clearly and concisely, and may have a tendency to interrupt or sound angry if they feel they are not getting their meaning across. As a result, they often find themselves involved in emotional clashes with colleagues. (See Chapter 5 for more information on dyspraxic difficulties.)

An example of a person with such difficulties is Melissa who worked as a computer programmer. Because of her difficulty with learning work procedures, Melissa frequently needed to ask questions and to request that instructions be repeated. But her poor communication skills meant that this was no easy task for her. She tended to ramble off the point when asking a question, and had difficulty focussing on replies. Her colleagues became exasperated by her constant questions and she became defiant and stubborn. Her panic at not following what they said caused her often to interrupt them and appear rude. Eventually, Melissa withdrew and ceased to ask questions, which further hampered her work performance. She also had difficulty taking part in social conversations and soon became the 'office loner'.

I met with Melissa's line manager and the company's HR manager to try to find ways of addressing this situation. I explained to them that it was not just a case of Melissa improving her communication skills, but that sympathy and understanding was needed from her colleagues as well. The HR manager came up with a scheme which would have the dual purpose of helping Melissa develop communication skills and informing the rest of the staff about dyslexic and dyspraxic difficulties. His suggestion was that Melissa should give an informal talk to her colleagues, outlining her difficulties and suggesting ways in which other people could be helpful to her in dealing with them.

At first both Melissa and I felt unsure about this idea, thinking it might increase her stress. However, having advised the HR manager that we should not set a deadline for the talk, but wait until Melissa had had all the time she needed to prepare and practise, I found Melissa ready to take on the challenge. We practised her talk long and hard during our sessions, preparing the material and role-playing the presentation and the question-and-answer session. We concentrated particularly on such things as tone of voice, pace of delivery, body language, and eye gaze. When Melissa felt fully prepared, she did the presentation and it was a huge success. She was elated at having 'risen to the occasion' so successfully.

The knowledge that she could cope with such a demanding communication task made her feel more confident in coping with day-to-day interactions. Her colleagues, too, enjoyed the presentation and felt they had gained much understanding from it. She is now much more engaged with her workmates and her performance and motivation have improved.

Job interviews

Many dyslexic people find interviews stressful. Typically they will talk in a muddled way, often veering wildly off the point. They find it difficult to remember questions they are asked, but their lack of confidence prevents them from requesting that questions be repeated. Feelings of panic may stop them from collecting their thoughts calmly, and their replies may consequently be punctuated by long silences.

Interviewers need to be made aware of how severely a dyslexic person's fear and lack of confidence may prevent them from demonstrating their intelligence, knowledge, skills, and experience in an interview. Trainers can help by speaking to interviewers on a client's behalf, prior to the date of the interview. Some helpful things which interviewers can be asked to do are:

- Encourage the person to request repetition of questions.
- Allow them a longer time to formulate replies.
- If any reading is needed during an interview, allow extra time for this, or give the reading in advance. (For more suggestions, see Information point B.)

By contrast, a confident dyslexic person can use an interview to show how well they cope with their difficulties. One dyslexic interviewee,

Rosalind, was applying for a job, and knew that in the interview she might have trouble explaining just how her dyslexic difficulties affected her and how she usually dealt with them. Before the interview, therefore, she prepared a clear one-page summary of her difficulties, her coping strategies, and the type of support that would be helpful for her. She sent this to the interviewers before the date of the interview. As she then felt confident that her interviewers would understand her situation, this substantially reduced her anxiety during the interview. She not only got the job but also was commended by the interviewers for her initiative and foresight in preparing a written note of her difficulties.

Work reviews

Work reviews can be particularly stressful for dyslexic employees. The review process tends to highlight the negative effects of their difficulties on their work performance – and this may well prevent the employee from achieving a satisfactory grade or earning a salary rise.

In work reviews, a dyslexia-savvy interviewer will not only be considering whether a dyslexic employee has met particular targets, but will also be considering, among other things, whether management could help the employee by setting lower targets, or giving the employee a longer time to reach them.

One of my clients had not had a merit rise for several years because his dyslexic difficulties had prevented him from fully meeting his performance goals. I spoke to his managers, who agreed it would be appropriate to reduce his targets until he had completed his training sessions with me. As a result, he was at last able to get his elusive merit rise – which gave a huge boost to his confidence, his motivation and, subsequently, his performance. The managers also agreed that his progress in our sessions should itself be included in his work targets for his next year's appraisal, giving him a better chance of meeting the criteria again.

Training courses

Workplace training courses can feel like a nightmare to dyslexic employees, mainly because trainers rarely know about dyslexia or how to make their courses dyslexia friendly. Training materials are often not presented in a way that is easy for dyslexic people to follow. Trainers may speak too quickly and not present their lectures in a clearly structured form. The courses are often intensive, and so dyslexic people find it hard to maintain concentration. They feel they are trailing behind the others on the course, and this makes them embarrassed and anxious. They are afraid to keep asking questions for fear of looking stupid in front of their colleagues. After one or two bad experiences on training courses, dyslexic employees often refuse to attend more courses, thereby ruining their prospects of promotion. Specialist trainers are, therefore, advised to liaise with workplace trainers to show them how to make their courses more dyslexia friendly. (For more suggestions on this, see Information point B.)

Teamwork

Working in teams can cause dyslexic employees a double anxiety: they feel nervous about having to perform in front of other people, and they fear letting down their team. Some organizations aim to improve staff motivation by organizing staff into competing teams and awarding prizes to the best-performing teams. In such a situation, however supportive and understanding the other team members may be, they are unlikely to react well if they see their team's achievement routinely pulled down by a dyslexic team-mate. In the case of one of my clients, a talk with a manager resolved such a problem by the manager agreeing to set a reduced target – not only for the dyslexic employee, but also for the team as a whole.

Dyslexic Strengths

Dyslexic people do face numerous difficulties in the workplace, but they also bring to their work a diverse range of strengths and talents. Through years of experience of coping with their difficulties, they have often developed a fighting spirit that reveals itself in great determination, tenacity, and motivation. They will often be extremely conscientious and willing to put in many extra hours to produce results. Often, too, they find creative ways to get around their problems, and consequently develop good lateral-thinking skills – skills which are sought after by many employers.

Further, if their dyslexic difficulties have not affected their oral skills, dyslexic people may develop extremely good interpersonal skills; they may shine in jobs which involve people management. Years of coping with their own difficulties have often made them sensitive and sympathetic to other people's needs and problems, and enabled them to develop a caring and considerate attitude to colleagues.

Finally, as shown in the case studies in this chapter, dyslexic people can find ways to tackle their anger, anxiety, frustration, and other negative emotions. If managers offer appropriate support, understanding, and sympathy, a dyslexic employee can succeed in being 'happy in his work'.

Conclusion

All of the difficult emotions and attitudes described in this chapter can cause problems at work – and some of them indeed can cause havoc. If left to 'fester', these problems can spread their tentacles into almost every aspect of working life, and into areas of an organization outside a dyslexic employee's immediate department. (For an example, see Chapter 1, pages 12–17.)

As well as affecting the day-to-day aspects of a person's job, dyslexic difficulties can interfere with job interviews, work reviews, workplace meetings, teamwork, and general interaction with colleagues. They can cause problems for workplace training and can hinder promotion opportunities. They can also mar interactions with customers and clients, which can sometimes be costly for an employer.

Sometimes the difficulties turn into disputes, and draw in HR managers and union representatives. Indeed the difficulties of a single employee, if not recognized and properly addressed, can result in hundreds of hours and thousands of pounds being spent in futile attempts to deal with grievances on the side of both employee and employer. From all this, it is clear that dyslexia trainers must be as adept at dealing with emotional issues as they are at offering training in particular workplace skills.

CHAPTER 11

Dyslexia on Trial

Melanie Jameson

Introduction

For adults with dyslexia, involvement in legal processes can present insuperable difficulties. The skills needed for coping with legal professionals, official documentation, and court or tribunal hearings are the very skills which dyslexic people often lack. Moreover, their inability to 'perform' as expected in interviews or court hearings may cast doubt on their integrity and prejudice their case.

Recently, at a meeting of a focus group convened by the former Disability Rights Commission, I facilitated a session on tribunals and courts where we considered the skills necessary for coping with hearings and legal processes. The group included adults with dyslexia, dyspraxia, attention deficit disorder, and Asperger's syndrome – conditions covered by the term 'specific learning difficulties' – and the list of skills they produced was as follows:

- Good oral communication.
- Understanding the import of questioning and responding appropriately.
- Ability to locate and respond impromptu to written information.
- Focused listening.
- Concentration and freedom from distractibility.
- Rapid information-processing skills.
- Accurate recall.

Dyslexia and Employment Edited by Sylvia Moody
© 2009 John Wiley & Sons, Ltd

• Consistency.
• Ability to cope with stress.

It is self-evident that people with specific learning difficulties will be greatly disadvantaged in situations, such as interviews and court hearings, which place heavy demands on speaking and listening skills and the efficient processing of information. Weakness in another key area – working memory – will inhibit performance during police interviews and preparation sessions with lawyers as well as in court and tribunal hearings. A person's credibility might be questioned if they seem to be hesitant or inconsistent; and they may appear evasive when they are simply missing the point of questions – and this is all too easy when questions are complex or when the individual is finding it increasingly hard to stay focused.

The Extent of the Problem

My first experience of supporting a dyslexic person in court left me appalled at the way the system worked. I had been asked to provide information on dyslexia in a magistrates' court on behalf of a member of my local Adult Dyslexia group. The way the hearing was conducted convinced me that the justice system is almost certain to fail people with dyslexia and related conditions. Neither lawyers, nor court officials nor the judiciary had even the most basic awareness of the effects of specific learning difficulties.

Subsequently, I became involved at a more formal level in a number of cases, and was asked to consider particular questions formulated by solicitors relating to the dyslexic difficulties of their clients. I was often required to appear as an expert witness and face cross-examination. I would always submit information on relevant aspects of the individual's specific learning difficulties prior to the hearing and propose accommodations in line with disability legislation. *However, time and time again, the impact of these difficulties was not taken into account by the legal professionals concerned.*

In one instance, I witnessed the acute problems that arise when someone appears before the courts without legal representation. This may happen in cases where legal aid has been unavailable or has been withdrawn at some point during the legal process. The result is that those least able to represent themselves are obliged to do so. Known as Unrepresented Parties or Litigants in Person, they face a double handicap: unfamiliarity with legal procedures and the impact of their specific learning difficulty.

Two case studies will illustrate the predicaments that can arise when dyslexic difficulties are misunderstood or meet with ignorance and lack of sympathy. One case had a successful outcome, the other foundered. Some key issues arising out of the two scenarios will be discussed.

These two cases presented a challenge to me as well as to my clients, as I felt I was starting virtually from scratch in finding ways to inform legal professionals, and in some cases the police, about the ways specific learning difficulties would disadvantage a person in interviews and in court. In the final section of this paper, I will outline the steps I have taken to promote a better understanding of such difficulties throughout the legal profession. Legal professionals will find extra information in the form of guidelines in Information point I.

Case Study 1: Guilty as Charged?

How a dyspraxic man narrowly escaped getting a criminal record

Background

Simon Jones, a site manager at a power station, is dyslexic and dyspraxic. While driving to work one morning, he exceeded the speed limit and was stopped by the police. He was asked to use the breathalyzer and, to his surprise, found himself quite unable to do so – he kept sucking on the device rather than blowing into it. After several unsuccessful attempts, he was charged not only with speeding but with the far more serious offence of obstructing the police.

He was taken to the police station where once again he was asked to blow into the breathalyzer – but again he found he could only suck on it. The charge stood. Simon saw the duty solicitor but could not take in all the procedural details which were explained to him. He could, however, grasp the main point: that he would have to plead guilty and so would now have a criminal record after a lifetime of good citizenship. He was released on bail.

On returning home, Simon telephoned me. It took me some time to unravel the facts from the garbled account of events that he gave me. I then recommended that he should change his plea to not guilty so that the case would have to come to trial. His defence would be that he did not wilfully refuse to comply with the police request about the breathalyzer; on the contrary he was trying his best to blow into it, but the combined effects of his dyspraxia, and the stress he was under at the time, were the reason for the apparently 'obstructive' behaviour.

I prepared for the case by conducting a detailed literature search for the effects of stress on dyslexia and dyspraxia and by drawing up a document which set out the full range of dyslexic and dyspraxic difficulties – this was to dispel the perception that they are simply problems with literacy. I had several sessions with Simon to ensure that I had gathered all the relevant information about the incident itself. Although we had known each other for a number of years, Simon found the interviews with me distressing because he was now in a continuous state of anxiety. He became so garrulous and inconsequential in his discourse that I began to wonder how he would be able to stand up to cross-examination in court.

The hearing

The hearing took place 2 months later at the local magistrates' court. We had to wait for over an hour, which was stressful for both of us as we had little idea of what to expect. Simon was called into court first; I was sent for about half-an-hour later to affirm my credentials and take questions from a representative of the Crown Prosecution Service.

It quickly became apparent that this case was regarded as a waste of court time; there was a presumption that Simon was guilty. My explanation of the likely effects of dyspraxia and dyslexia initially met with incredulity (although my documentation on this matter had been submitted in advance, as required). However, I had carefully backed up all my claims with research evidence, and, as a result, the prosecution decided to shift ground.

I was suddenly asked about Simon's ability to drive! It was suggested that this ability might be impaired, given that he could easily become stressed and fail to process information efficiently. Fortunately, I knew that Simon was an excellent driver and that he had passed the advanced driving test.

Mention was also made of inconsistencies in the information Simon had supplied to the police, and of what was perceived as his evasiveness in successive interview sessions. However, the information which I had submitted on Simon's difficulties clearly highlighted his poor short-term and working memory, his short attention span, and his impaired ability to grasp what was required of him when he was tired and overloaded with information. Simon's solicitor was therefore able to argue persuasively that the inconsistencies and evasiveness were not deliberate, but were the result of his dyslexic difficulties.

The issue at the heart of the matter, namely, Simon's non-compliance during repeated breathalyzer tests, was next in the frame. I tackled this matter by presenting evidence about the effects of stress on physical coordination.

When the Prosecutor resumed his questioning of Simon, it became apparent that Simon had at this point suffered 'mental overload'. Normally outgoing, cheerful, and talkative, he was now almost speechless. He had to ask for every question to be repeated and was continually asked to speak up when giving his hesitant responses. Nevertheless the evidence was on our side and he won his case. After the event Simon's comment was: 'I went completely to pot there. What happened in the end?'

Sting in the tail

Despite the successful outcome of the case, Simon's problems were still not over. The police wrote to the DVLC expressing a concern about Simon's fitness to drive due to the fact that he experienced 'episodes of confusion'. (Anyone experiencing such 'episodes' is required to have a re-appraisal of their entitlement to hold a driver's licence.) Asked by Simon's solicitor to compose a response, I wrote a letter explaining that the term 'episodes of confusion' required clarification in the case of Simon. I explained that, as a result of his dyslexia, he could in certain circumstances become confused when completing forms, dialling telephone numbers, and following instructions. I stressed that none of this had any bearing on his ability as a driver. Nothing more was heard about the withdrawal of Simon's driving licence.

The effect of this episode on Simon was that he completely lost confidence in himself. He had found the court appearance traumatic. The effect it had on me was to make me feel more determined to find a way to raise awareness about specific learning difficulties amongst the legal profession, the police service, and the judiciary.

Comment

This case showed

- how stress can combine with dyslexic/dyspraxic difficulties to cause a person to be perceived as being obstructive when this is not their intention;
- how little the police and legal professions understand about specific learning difficulties;
- how prosecutors can 'shift their ground' during cross-examination, and raise unexpected and threatening issues.

Reflecting after the case on what else I could have done to support Simon, I thought that I might perhaps have tried to obtain a rest break in order to restore Simon's ability to concentrate. However, I doubt if this would have been granted because, at the time of the hearing, Part III of the Disability Discrimination Act (which obliges the courts to take account of the needs of people with disabilities) had not yet come into force.

If I had known that Simon had been arrested, I would certainly have gone along to the police station to see if I could have offered him support, given that, under the Police and Criminal Evidence Act, someone who could have difficulty coping with police questioning has the right to be accompanied by an 'appropriate adult'.

Even though Part III of the Act is now in force, the situation for people with specific learning difficulties has scarcely improved as regards courts or tribunal hearings. I have recently studied the judicial handbook (the Equal Treatment Bench Book) to ascertain what guidance this provides: there are revised sections on Mental Disability and Mental Capacity, covering individuals with generalized learning difficulties/disabilities, but information on specific learning difficulties is completely lacking.

It is my belief that, for roughly 10% of the population, access to justice cannot be assured until awareness of specific learning difficulties has been disseminated throughout the judiciary, the police, and the legal profession.

Case Study 2: In the Hands of the Experts

How a dyslexic woman despaired of getting justice

In this case, it was the dyslexic plaintiff's own solicitors and the medical specialists in the case who caused the difficulties.

Background

Tracy Williams worked as a hairdresser and was in her early 50s. She lacked formal qualifications in her profession but had many years of experience. She had been diagnosed as dyslexic 4 years previously. At the time she contacted me, Tracy was in dispute with her employer. Following a whiplash injury, she had asked permission to work on a high stool rather than standing, but this had been refused – in fact her employer had stated that, if she could not work standing like her colleagues, she would have to leave the job. Tracy felt that this was 'unfair dismissal' and decided to take her employer to an employment tribunal. She engaged a solicitor and was asked to undertake further medical examinations.

Meeting the professionals

Ensuing meetings with solicitors and medical experts caused Tracy unexpected problems which she attributed to her dyslexia. She telephoned me for help and advice and I asked her to send me a written account of the difficulties she had been experiencing. The letter I received from her did not shed a flattering light on the professionals involved in her case. Tracy began:

> I have found the whole legal and medical process in connection with my accident and unfair dismissal claims extremely complex and stressful. This has been compounded by my dyslexia, and I am now suffering from bouts of depression. I have tried – and failed – to make my solicitor aware of dyslexia and how it affects me, but have found her very unsympathetic. Also, the medical examinations and interviews I've had with specialists (on both sides) have been extremely distressing.
>
> Attempts to explain my dyslexia have often been met with remarks about successful celebrity dyslexics, such as Duncan Goodhew or Richard Branson, pointing out how well they've done. The

> suggestion seems to be that I am a failure. Consequently, I feel I have not been able to give a clear account of the events leading up to my unfair dismissal claim, and their impact on my life. I feel very aware that those I'm dealing with have little or no understanding of, or respect for, my disability. I find the whole process both exhausting and dispiriting.

And it got worse. One of the solicitors who became involved claimed to know about dyslexia but began the interview with the remark 'I gather you have a dodgy memory'; this undermined Tracy's confidence for the rest of the meeting. She felt she was being bullied and bombarded by questions, allowed no space to give thoughtful replies, and no time to consult the notes she had made on the sequence of events leading up to the claim. In the subsequent medical examination Tracy had similar experiences. She found it difficult to make her points clearly and eventually became tongue-tied. The specialist then told her that she was entitled to abandon the examination if she wished. This simply added to her anxiety as she felt that this would look as if she was being uncooperative.

Dyslexia under suspicion

Tracy started to get the impression that the specialists thought she was using dyslexia as an excuse. At one stage she had sight of a report which read:

> During the interview with Ms Williams it was often impossible to obtain a clear history . . . she appeared to have difficulty comprehending the questions posed and frequently asked 'what do you mean?' She seemed extremely anxious ... (she) gave a history which was extremely confusing and often blamed this on the dyslexia and short-term memory.

I felt shocked by the total lack of knowledge, sensitivity, and courtesy shown by the doctors and solicitors involved in the case. I was already aware of the vulnerability of dyslexic people during hearings but had not previously realized how difficult and distressing the preparation stage could also be.

By now the Dispute Resolution Procedure, in which a document passes between employer and employee, had been instigated. Although Tracy pointed out on several occasions that she found form filling difficult and intimidating, she received no official assistance with this task. Having struggled to supply the necessary details, she began to worry that some of her responses might be inaccurate because she might have misunderstood questions which seemed ambiguous.

Visual stress

Tracy's difficulties with written materials were compounded by visual stress, a problem which causes text to appear blurred or distorted. (For further information on visual stress, see Information point E.) This caused Tracy particular embarrassment when documentation was placed in front of her for comment during an interview. Being acutely conscious of her reading difficulties and the poor impression she was making, she became ever more stressed and her dyslexic difficulties became correspondingly more severe.

General stress

Tracy described her reaction to the situation at this point in these words:

> There seems to be little or no recognition that the legal and medical processes are causing me extreme stress because of difficulties stemming from my dyslexia (especially information overload, poor memory, difficulty putting my views over, low self-esteem and lack of confidence). These affect my ability to make my case clearly.
>
> I have found the manner of some of the specialists at times both unprofessional and patronising. They have shown a complete lack of sensitivity.

An unhappy ending

As it became clear that the employer was not prepared to cooperate with the Resolution Procedure, an employment tribunal hearing was arranged. I met with Tracy to explain that I could supply information on her dyslexia that would authenticate her difficulties; I said that I would approach this by listing her difficulties (as described in her assessment report), establishing that these amounted to a disability under the terms of the Disability Discrimination Act, and proposing reasonable adjustments that the court should take into account. The resulting document was drafted with Tracy, drawn up and forwarded to her solicitor.

Unfortunately it was too late to rescue the situation. Tracy had given up. As she explained in a further letter to me:

> My confidence in the whole process, and in particular in the individuals involved, has disintegrated. I am very concerned that I will not be able to put my views over as I would wish in the forthcoming hearing. I am afraid that I will be unable to grasp what the questions are seeking to establish and will do myself down.

She withdrew from the case, left the job and tried to get work elsewhere.

Comment

Clearly, it was not sufficient simply to seek to inform those involved in the *hearing* itself of the nature of dyslexic difficulties: documentation on these should have been presented to all the professionals involved in the case *at every stage*. There is obviously much to be done before awareness of specific learning difficulties is disseminated throughout the legal profession. In the meantime, perhaps we should suggest that anyone with dyslexia who is engaged in preparing a case should be accompanied to meetings by someone from their local dyslexia association who could not only help them with notetaking and locating information, but also explain dyslexic difficulties to the professionals involved.

Discussion

The two cases described above brought home to me how vulnerable people with specific learning difficulties are at the hands of ignorant – and sometimes patronizing – professionals, even when these professionals are actually meant to be on their side. Recent work as an expert witness and advisor to disability organizations has only confirmed me in the view that the problems experienced by people with specific learning difficulties who come before courts and tribunals are neither understood nor accommodated – despite the fact that the courts are included in Part III of the Disability Discrimination Act on the provision of services to the public.

This lack of awareness and understanding can be particularly serious in cases of offenders with dyslexia who are found to be for a second time in breach of the terms of their community orders and are returned to the courts. In many instances, these breaches appear to arise out of dyslexic difficulties such as poor organization. Unfortunately, these shortcomings are not generally viewed sympathetically by the courts who may hand down custodial sentences.

Ways Forward

For some time, I could not see a way forward in raising dyslexia awareness amongst legal professionals. Fortunately, however, a route has recently presented itself to me in the form of an opportunity to collaborate with a senior judge who is in charge of disability issues. At his suggestion, I have written a section on Specific Learning Difficulties for the handbook called Equal Treatment Bench Book, which circulates to all judges, magistrates, and tribunal chairs. At the time of going to press, this new section has been favourably received by the Equal Treatment Advisory Committee which oversees this work. To reinforce this initiative, it is hoped that a scenario featuring someone with dyslexia will be included in the next batch of training materials for the judiciary. Finally, I have an invitation to make a presentation on Specific Learning Difficulties and the Courts to the Equal Treatment Advisory Committee. It is hoped that this three-pronged approach will bear fruit.

However, success in updating judicial guidance is not the whole answer. This issue must also be taken on board by the Ministry of Justice and reflected in their Disability Equality Scheme, through which they take account of the needs of people with disabilities, including both their employees and users of their services. Provisions should include a widening of the remit of Disability Liaison Officers, who act as a source of information for both court users and professionals. These officials need good awareness training in respect of specific learning difficulties. Pre-court visits and pre-trial planning for people with dyslexia should be the norm, reasonable adjustments should be put in place as necessary, and assistance should be made available during hearings.

In order to disseminate awareness beyond the judiciary and throughout the whole justice system, it is necessary to extend this work also to lawyers through their lead body, the Law Society. The Society's committee which is responsible for equality and disability issues has a responsibility to promote an understanding of the problems faced in the courts by people with specific learning difficulties, and to embed this knowledge in the training of all solicitors and barristers. The Police, the Crown Prosecution Service, and the Youth Justice Board must also come on board. Only then can we hope to achieve the aim clearly stated in the Equal Treatment Bench Book, namely: 'To ensure that disability does not amount to a handicap to the attainment of justice'.

INFORMATION POINT H

Disability Discrimination Legislation

Brenda Allan

Legislation passed in the last 12 years has been designed to prevent discrimination against people with a disability, whether they are the recipients of services or in employment. The main relevant legislation is as follows:

- Disability Discrimination Act 1995 (DDA)
- Disability Discrimination Act (DDA) 2005
- Special Educational Needs and Disability Act 2001 (SENDA)
- Council Directive (2000/78/EEC) 27 November 2000, establishing a general framework for equal treatment in relation to employment and occupation

Discrimination and Employment

The DDA (2005) applies to all employers in the United Kingdom, with the sole exception of the armed forces, regardless of the number of their employees.

The DDA covers employees, contract workers, office holders, and business partners. Volunteers are not generally covered but can be if they receive a fee (and are not simply reclaiming expenses or other employment benefit such as training).

The combined effect of the legislation is to prohibit discrimination in the employment of disabled people at all stages of the employment process, including recruitment, training, promotion, benefits, and

Dyslexia and Employment Edited by Sylvia Moody
© 2009 John Wiley & Sons, Ltd

dismissal. It also prohibits discrimination by trade organizations and qualifications bodies. The legislation provides procedures for enforcement and the provision of remedies if discrimination occurs.

Provision of Good Service and Facilities

The legislation requires service providers to make reasonable adjustments for disabled people accessing a service.

Promoting Equality

The 2005 DDA introduced a duty on all public bodies to promote equality of opportunity for disabled people. This means that they must take account of the needs of disabled people as an integral part of their policies, practices, and procedures, and not as something separate or additional. They will have to have due regard to the need to

- eliminate unlawful discrimination and disability-related harassment.
- promote equality of opportunity and positive attitudes to disabled people.
- encourage disabled people to participate in public life.

Definition of Disability

'A person has a disability for the purposes of this Act if he/she has a *physical or mental impairment* which has a *substantial* and *long-term* adverse effect on his ability to carry out his *normal day-to-day activities*' (*Section 1 of the 1995 Act Schedule 1*).

Type of disability/impairment

The definition of a disabled person includes the following:

- People with long-term health conditions such as diabetes.
- People with progressive conditions such as multiple sclerosis (from the point of diagnosis rather than the point when the condition has

some adverse affect on their ability to carry out normal day-to-day activities).

- People who have been diagnosed with HIV or cancer (again from the point of diagnosis).
- People with learning disabilities.
- People with mental health conditions (from 2005 without the requirement that these must be 'clinically well recognized').
- People who have mobility impairments.
- Blind and partially sighted people.
- Deaf and hearing-impaired people.

Duration of disability

The duration of the disability needs to have a long-term, adverse effect that has lasted, or is likely to last, more than 12 months.

Degree of disability

The disability needs to have a substantial effect. In the Guidance (A1), the meaning of a substantial adverse effect is defined as one that is greater than would be produced by the sort of physical or mental conditions which many people experience and which have only minor effects. A substantial effect is one which is *more than minor or trivial.*

The *time taken* by a person with an impairment to carry out a normal day-to-day activity should be considered when assessing whether the effect of that impairment is substantial. It should be compared with the time that might be expected if the person did not have the impairment. (A2.)

Another factor to be considered when assessing whether the effect of a disability is substantial is *the way in which a person with that disability carries out* a normal day-to-day activity. The comparison should be with the way the person might be expected to carry out the activity if he did not have the disability. (A3).

Day-to-day activities

An impairment is to be taken to affect the ability of the person concerned to carry out normal day-to-day activities only if it affects one of the following:

- Mobility.
- Manual dexterity.
- Physical coordination.
- Continence.
- Ability to lift, carry, or otherwise move day-to-day objects.
- Speech, hearing, or eyesight.
- Memory or ability to concentrate, learn, or understand.
- Perception of the risk of physical danger.
  (Paragraph 4 (1) Schedule 1 of the 1995 Act)

The difficulties arising from dyslexia fall under the paragraph relating to memory or ability to concentrate, learn, or understand.

Part C of the Guidance provides the following clarification of day-to-day activities:

> The term normal day-to-day activities is not intended to include activities which are normal only for a particular person or group of people. Therefore, in deciding whether an activity is a normal day-to-day activity, account should be taken of how far it is normal for most people and carried out by most people on a daily or frequent and fairly regular basis. (C2).

However, since the passing of the different pieces of legislation, there have been varying interpretations of this by employment tribunals and employment appeal tribunals which have further clarified definitions. For example, in one case, it was observed that if an impairment is of the kind described in Para 4 of Schedule 1, it would be almost inevitable that it would have an adverse affect on normal day-to-day activities (*Ekpe v Metropolitan Police Commissioner (2001) ICR 1084 Para 30*). So, if an impairment affected someone's memory or ability to concentrate, learn, or understand, it would be very likely that this would have an adverse effect on normal day-to-day activities.

Additionally, there has been further clarification of what constitutes day-to-day activities. A recent case (Patterson v Commissioner of Police for the Metropolis 237207) involved an appeal by a police officer who experienced difficulties performing in the assessment tests required for promotion. Broadly, the employment tribunal found that passing promotion tests was not a day-to-day activity. However, the appeal tribunal found that, once it was accepted that the officer's disability affected his ability to achieve promotion, the disability therefore had a substantial effect on his day-to-day activities. They argued that any other conclusion would mean that because of his dyslexia, he would in practice face a glass ceiling, and this would frustrate one of the intentions of the legislation, which is to prevent discrimination with respect to the opportunities an employer affords a disabled person for promotion.

In making its decision the appeal tribunal also stated that it was for the tribunal, not the expert witness, to decide what constituted day-to-day activities and whether the adverse effect of a disability was substantial.

Coping strategies

There are certain provisions in the legislation which deal with coping strategies. In some cases, coping strategies will prevent an impairment having adverse effects, but they should be taken into account only where they can be relied upon in *all* circumstances (A8). In some cases, people have coping strategies which cease to work in certain circumstances (e.g. where someone who stutters or has dyslexia is placed under stress). If it is possible that a person's ability to manage the effects of an impairment will break down so that effects will sometimes still occur, this possibility must be taken into account when assessing the effects of the impairment.

Meaning of Discrimination

An employer is deemed to discriminate against a disabled person if the employer

- treats that person less favourably than they would treat others;
- cannot show that the treatment was justified;
- fails to comply with a duty of reasonable adjustment imposed by the DDA.

Less favourable treatment of a disabled person will only be justified if the reason for it is both material, that is, relevant to the circumstances of the particular case and substantial, that is, not trivial. The Code of Practice Relating to Employment (published by the Department of Education and Employment UK, 1966) says that less favourable treatment will be justified if the disabled person cannot do the job concerned, and that no adjustment which would enable a person to do the job (or another vacant job) is practicable.

Education

This is relevant to employees who may be pursuing full-time or part-time education courses. The Special Educational Needs Discrimination Act (SENDA) extends the provisions of the 1995 DDA into education. The Act places responsibilities on local authorities, universities, and colleges to ensure that disabled students are not treated less favourably than others as a result of their disability. The Act imposes a duty to make reasonable adjustments so that disabled students are not put at a substantial disadvantage compared to others. For colleges and universities, less favourable treatment can be justified if it is necessary to maintain academic standards.

Universities and colleges are required to provide auxiliary aids and services where appropriate and need to consider altering premises, if necessary.

Advice Organization

Equality and Human Rights Commission (www.equalityhumanrights.com).

CHAPTER 12

How to Write a Legal Report

Sylvia Moody

This chapter gives guidance on writing a diagnostic dyslexia report in a legal format. Such a report will include information on the nature of dyslexic difficulties, your opinion on the *specific* questions the solicitor has asked (his/her 'instructions'), and the theoretical background on which you rely in formulating your opinion.

Below, I will first suggest a recommended report structure in outline, and then discuss each section in detail.

Outline of the Report Structure

1. Title page
2. Structure of report
3. Reason for report
4. Qualifications
5. Summary
6. Basis of report
7. Background
8. Previous assessments
9. Interview
10. Tests done and summary of results
11. Theoretical issues
12. Opinion
13. Declaration

© 2009 John Wiley & Sons, Ltd

Appendix A: curriculum vitae
Appendix B: documents you have read in preparing the report
Appendix C: test results in detail
Appendix D: tests used
Appendix E: references
Additional letter (optional): recommendations for a training programme

Detailed Notes on the Content of the Report

In this section, I shall illustrate various points by 'quoting' from a hypothetical case: Mr Jones, a dyslexic employee (the Plaintiff) against his employer, Wray Translations Ltd (the Defendant). Mr Jones is suing his employer for discriminating against him because of his dyslexia. His solicitors are called Deacon Groves.

1. Title page

This should include your contact details, the name of the report, for example, *Diagnostic Dyslexia Assessment of Peter Jones*, the client's date of birth, the date of the assessment, the solicitor's reference, and your reference.

2. Structure of report

It is helpful for solicitors to see the structure of your report before reading it, so you could put the report outline (shown above) on the second page.

3. Reason for report

Here you explain who instructed you (i.e. commissioned you to do the report), and give the *exact instructions* that you have been given.

> Deacon Groves, Solicitors, have requested that I see Mr Jones for a dyslexia assessment. In particular, they have asked me to state whether, in my opinion:

1. Mr Jones suffers from dyslexia.
2. If so, what is the extent/severity of his condition.
   In particular, do his difficulties affect his ability to carry out normal day-to-day activities.
3. What adjustments would it be appropriate for Wray Translations to make in order to take account of Mr Jones' difficulties.

Note: Everything that follows in the report must be relevant to these instructions and not stray into areas which these instructions do not cover.

4. Qualifications

Here you just need to put a very brief paragraph to give some idea of your background. Leave your full CV to an appendix.

5. Summary

This again is just a few lines' summary of the opinion that you have formulated, so that the Court can see at a glance what you have concluded:

> Mr Jones is a man of above-average intellectual ability who has dyslexic difficulties, some of which are severe. These difficulties do constitute a mental impairment. They are long-standing and have had an adverse effect on his ability to carry out day-to-day activities, as well as on his work performance. There are a number of adjustments his employer could be asked to make to accommodate his difficulties.

Note: It is usually best not to use 'comprehensive' phrases such as 'his dyslexia is severe' as different components of a dyslexic syndrome may be at different levels of severity – for example, visual tracking may be extremely poor, while short-term memory may be relatively strong.

6. Basis of the report

This explains what evidence you have taken into account in formulating your opinion, for example, test results, information received from the client, information received from the employer, and so on.

> This report is based on information gained from previous reports on Mr Jones, information from Wray Translations (as reported by Deacon Groves), an interview with Mr Jones, and the administration to him of psychological tests and questionnaires.

7. Background

This is the factual background to the case: how and why the case came about. This can usually be taken largely from the initial letter that the solicitor sends you with his/her instructions. This letter will probably also have information about how the employer and employee respectively view the situation. *You should make it completely clear in this section when you are quoting opinions from the employer/employee, and when you are reporting factual information provided by the solicitor.*

(a) Reason for the case being brought

> According to information received from Deacon Groves, Mr Jones has been employed by Wray Translations since June 2006. He is taking his employer to an Employment Tribunal for the following reasons
>
> They are refusing to acknowledge that he is a disabled person under the Disability Discrimination Act 1995.
> They have discriminated against him because of his disability/dyslexia.
> They have failed to make reasonable adjustments, as required by the DDA.

(b) Nature of Mr Jones' job

> Mr Jones began work as Service Control Administrator in June 2006. This position involves monitoring and analyzing calls and call trends, and corresponding with customers.

(c) Employer's concerns

> According to the information given by Wray Translations in their Defence, and the Disciplinary Meeting Notes of 24 October 2007, the following aspects of Mr Jones' work gave persistent cause for concern: frequent mistakes, failure to prioritize, failing to meet deadlines.

8. Previous assessment(s)

Include here any relevant information from previous psychological reports. You may also wish to note relevant information given in medical reports, for example, diagnoses of depression and/or physical conditions which could exacerbate dyslexic difficulties.

9. Interview

First, give the circumstances of the interview:

> I saw Mr Jones at my consulting room, on 15 January 2008. Mr Jones was fully cooperative, and the results of the assessment are considered reliable.

Then, report everything that you have learned from your interview/assessment. It is important to include the client's own report of his/her difficulties, and how he/she feels the employer has responded. This can be contrasted later, if relevant, with the employer's view of the situation (given in Section 7c 'Employer's concerns').

Note: In the section on difficulties reported by the client, it is *essential to include day-to-day difficulties*. (You will find relevant questionnaires in Appendix A.) Under the Disability Discrimination Act, it is day-to-day difficulties which the Court takes into account when deciding whether a person is disabled.

10. Tests used and test results in summary

Here you describe the tests you have used and give a summary of the test results. It is not appropriate here to give your opinion on what the results signify; this will be given later in the Opinion section. Nor is it useful to give detailed results of your test scores: these can go in an appendix.

11. Theoretical issues

This is a very important section. You need to make clear the theoretical basis of your Opinion, and to show that you have given full consideration to conflicting definitions of, and theories about, dyslexia.

It is useful to lay out this section in numbered paragraphs, so that in the following section, when you give your Opinion, you can keep referring back to the relevant theoretical issues. Below are examples of two paragraphs which are generally useful in dyslexia assessment reports.

(a) Description of dyslexia

Dyslexia is often regarded simply as a difficulty with reading and spelling, but in fact poor literacy is usually just one of a number of 'signs and symptoms' which are associated with a syndrome of underlying cognitive deficits, notably weaknesses in verbal short-term memory, phonological abilities, and speed of information processing. Other dyslexic 'signs' are poor organizational skills, difficulty in expressing oneself succinctly, and a general difficulty with tasks which depend on sequencing and structure (Turner, 1997; Singleton, 1999; Bartlett and Moody, 2000a, b; Reid and Kirk 2000 a, b; Fitzgibbon and O'Connor, 2002; Grant, 2002; McLoughlin et al., 2002; Moody, 2006).

(b) Assessment criteria for dyslexia

In general assessors look for three strands of evidence:

1. A discrepancy between intellectual ability and literacy level.
2. Specific cognitive weaknesses (e.g. in short-term memory, phonological processing).
3. Poor literacy skills, especially slow reading of words and non-words, slow writing, and difficulty in reading for comprehension and in structuring written work. (It is important that the literacy tests used

in an assessment are appropriate for adults, are wide ranging in scope, *and include speed tests.* Tests of single-word reading and spelling alone are inadequate.)

If all three of the above are found, it is unlikely that a dyslexia diagnosis would be disputed (McLoughlin et al., 1997; Turner, 1997; Singleton, 1999; Bartlett and Moody, 2000a, b; Moody, 2001a; Reid and Kirk, 2001a, b; Fitzgibbon and O'Connor, 2002; Grant, 2002; McLoughlin et al., 2002; Moody, 2006).

Note: The reason why I include information about appropriate tests under point 3 is that it often happens that a client has had a previous – inadequate – assessment in which tests of *single-word* reading and spelling alone were used, and on the basis of this assessment, the client has been found to be 'not dyslexic'. So it is important in such cases for the Court to understand why you think that a previous assessment was inadequate.

12. Opinion

In this section, you finally give your answers to the questions which the solicitor had asked in his/her instructions.

1. Is Mr Jones dyslexic?

   I consider Mr Jones to be dyslexic, that is, he has a mental impairment. He has a range of cognitive deficits and literacy difficulties which match the description of dyslexia given in Section 11a, and which further meet all three of the criteria for the identification of dyslexia listed in Section 11b.

2. Are his difficulties severe enough to affect daily life?

   Mr Jones' difficulties are severe enough to adversely affect his ability to carry out normal day-to-day activities. Examples of day-to-day activities which he finds difficult or impossible are: reading bank statements, filling in forms, writing a cheque.

Note: While each of the difficulties may individually be mild, they may cumulatively be severe enough to affect daily life.

3. What adjustments could his employer make?

His employer could allow him time off work for dyslexia tuition, provide IT support, and allow extra rest breaks.

13. Declaration

This is a standard text in which you declare yourself satisfied that the facts you have reported are true and the opinions you have expressed are correct. The solicitor will be able to give you the full text.

Appendix A: curriculum vitae

Put your detailed CV here. If you have training in giving evidence at tribunals and legal report writing, include this.

Appendix B

Documents you have read in preparing the report.

Appendix C

Test results in detail.

Appendix D

Tests used.

A brief description of the tests you have used, distinguishing, for instance, tests of reading accuracy from tests of reading speed and comprehension.

Appendix E

References.

Here you list the references that you have quoted in the Theoretical Issues section.

Additional letter (optional): recommendations for a training programme

Recommendations for a training programme may have been requested in the solicitor's instructions, in which case you will already have covered this in your report. If the instructions do not request such recommendations, you may feel that you would like to give your client relevant advice on an informal basis.

However, if you are retained by the employer, you might not be at liberty to divulge the results of your assessment or give advice about training to the employee at the time of the assessment. In this case, you could record your recommendations in the form of a letter and send this to the instructing solicitor, asking him/her to make the information available to the client at a suitable moment. Or you could advise the client that, when eventually the legal process is completely finished, he/she can contact you for advice on help and support.

Some General Considerations

As an expert witness, you are giving independent advice to the Court, not in any way 'taking sides' in a case. This might seem too obvious to state. However, in practice there can be a danger that an expert witness may unconsciously introduce bias into their reports. Here are two particular dangers to be alert to:

1. If you are an experienced dyslexia professional, you may probably have come to have great sympathy with dyslexic people and to feel indignant at the unsympathetic way they are often treated in the workplace. You could therefore find yourself slipping into the role of advocate rather than witness.
2. Cases take a long time to come to Court, and over that period you will have contact with the solicitor acting for the Plaintiff or Defendant. You could unconsciously be drawn into feeling that you are somehow on that solicitor's 'team', on his/her side.

When acting as an expert witness you may find opportunities to raise awareness among members of the legal profession about the difficulties that dyslexic people face when giving evidence in court. (See Information point I.)

INFORMATION POINT I

Specific Learning Difficulties: Guidelines for Lawyers

Melanie Jameson

In these guidelines, I will describe the difficulties experienced by people with specific learning difficulties in interviews with solicitors or police, and in court or tribunal hearings. I will also make suggestions for how these difficulties can be properly accommodated. I shall deal with three types of specific learning difficulties: dyslexia, dyspraxia, and attention deficit (hyperactivity) disorder, usually known as AD(H)D. First, a few general remarks.

Up to 10% of the population experience these three specific learning difficulties to a lesser or greater extent. The incidence is known to be far higher amongst offenders and is thought to be a factor in breaches of community orders. It is useful to draw attention, in particular, to the vulnerability of young people who have these difficulties. Having often grown up in circumstances which have made them socially isolated, they may easily be drawn into undesirable groups who are accepting of their difficulties, but lead them into criminal activities. The very nature of specific learning difficulties means that those who suffer from them are the ones most likely to be arrested, while other members of a group will escape. They may also be suggestible and this often results in them 'carrying the can' for the group as a whole.

Dyslexia

Dyslexia is associated with weaknesses in information processing, language skills, short-term memory, and organizational skills. People with

---

Dyslexia and Employment Edited by Sylvia Moody
© 2009 John Wiley & Sons, Ltd

dyslexia may also be subject to visual stress which makes it difficult for them to read text quickly. (For more information on visual stress, see Information point E.)

Dyspraxia

Dyspraxia has been described as an impairment in the planning, organization, and execution of actions. It can also impair organization of thought and sensory integration. Consequently, people with dyspraxia have difficulty in being succinct when they are speaking or writing, and, when they are reading, they may have difficulty in grasping the overall meaning of a text and get lost in detail.

Poor sensory integration leads to difficulty in coping in an environment where there are multiple stimulations and where different activities are being carried out simultaneously. Often there is a feeling of being overwhelmed by trying to comprehend complex information at the same time as executing demanding tasks, such as filling in a form. This can be compounded by sensory overload if lighting is too bright.

Attention Deficit (Hyperactivity) Disorder

People with AD(H)D are characterized by the following:

- *Difficulty in maintaining attention and concentration.* They have difficulty in focussing on tasks or listening for a sustained period of time, and are easily distracted by external stimuli. They may appear to be dreamy and 'mentally absent' for much of the time.
- *Impulsivity.* They may find it hard to inhibit impulses and this can show itself in the need for instant gratification. For instance, they may have difficulty taking turns in a conversation and might impatiently blurt out inappropriate comments.
- *Hyperactivity.* They are overactive – both physically and mentally. Associated traits include difficulty getting started on/finishing tasks, frequently losing or forgetting things, and being generally disorganized.

Some people have difficulties with attention, but are not impulsive or hyperactive. They are then simply said to have attention deficit disorder.

It is easy to see why people with ADHD could, in interview situations, appear to be uncooperative. They may seem to be not attending and failing to keep to the point in their replies; they may also cause annoyance by fidgeting and moving around incessantly, talking excessively, and intruding into other people's personal space.

Effects of Stress

Participation in courts or tribunals is particularly stressful for people with specific learning difficulties; this sets up a vicious circle, as their difficulties become significantly worse under stress.

In order to function in everyday life they will have built up an array of coping strategies which enable them to compensate for their difficulties; however, in a stressful situation, such as a court hearing, these strategies are likely to break down, leaving their difficulties 'exposed'. Furthermore, the fear that they are performing badly will heighten their anxiety, often to the degree that they come across as completely incompetent. Some people with dyslexia have reported that in stressful situations they also experience debilitating physical symptoms, such as queasiness, faintness, hyperventilation, and rapid heartbeat.

Good Practice

People with disabilities are entitled to have their needs considered and their difficulties accommodated, insofar as this is reasonable. This approach is enshrined in key pieces of legislation:

- The Disability Discrimination Act (1995) which stipulates that *reasonable adjustments* must be made for people who fit the definition of disability.
- The Human Rights Act (1998) which establishes the right to a fair trial.
- The Disability Equality Duty incumbent on the courts (2007).

These obligations can be met by provision of a document which

(a) details particular difficulties which an individual has (and which have been confirmed by a formal assessment);

(b) describes how these will impact on appearances before a court or tribunal;
(c) outlines the accommodations which could be made for them.

The guidelines given below give detailed information on

- the particular ways in which specific learning difficulties may manifest themselves in court;
- appropriate accommodations.

It is to be hoped that professionals involved in the justice system will take account of the proposed accommodations.

How Specific Learning Difficulties May Disadvantage People in Police and Legal Interviews and in Court

Difficulties arising from dyslexia, dyspraxia, and AD(H)D vary considerably from person to person, but the following problems are typical:

Memory

- Poor recall of dates and details of incidents (this may give the impression of unreliability).
- Problems estimating the passage of time (this could be important when giving evidence).
- Problems with remembering names (this could apply to people, places, or items such as drugs or medication).

Communication

- Difficulty in understanding oblique, implied, or complex questions.
- An inconsequential style of speaking that does not seem to keep to the point.
- Overloud and/or garrulous speech.
- Word-finding problems, leading to poor verbal expression.
- Mispronunciation of words.

Sequencing/orientation

- Difficulty presenting a sequence of events in a logical, structured way resulting in possible inconsistencies.
- Incorrect sequencing of number and letter strings (such as car number plates).
- Inaccurate references to left and right.

Literacy

- Even if reading skills are adequate, skimming through documentation or easily locating a piece of information in a court bundle could be difficult.
- Difficulty with reading because of visual stress. This can cause a person to see white paper as 'glaring' and print as being distorted. It may also cause eye strain and difficulty in keeping the place on the page. Visual stress can be exacerbated by fluorescent lighting.
- Erratic spelling and/or awkward or illegible handwriting.

Attention/emotion/concentration

- A limited attention span leading to mental overload and/or a high level of distractibility.
- Difficulty coping with background noise, bustle and, in some cases, bright lights.
- Particular susceptibility to the effects of stress.
- Appearing to be 'in a dream'.

Recommended Accommodations to be Made by Police Interviewers or Legal Professionals

When delivering spoken information

- Allow thinking time before pressing for a response.
- Allow the client to ask for questions to be repeated or re-phrased without censure or (implied) criticism. The client may need to check understanding by re-phrasing questions.

- When reading information out to a client, insert pauses after each section to allow the information to be absorbed.
- When providing complex information (such as explaining a person's rights) first introduce the topic, then give the details, then summarize if necessary.
- Check back to ensure understanding.
- Be aware of a likely limited attention span and the possibility of mental overload.

When delivering/referring to written information

- Be aware that some dyslexic people have considerable difficulty comprehending written material, despite being able to read adequately.
- If the client suffers from visual stress (see above), documentation for study or for reference in court should be adapted accordingly. Good practice is for written material to be well spaced and shown in a reasonable font size (not below 12 pt) and justified *left only*. Bright white paper should be avoided, and instead tinted paper, such as pale blue or grey, should be used.
- Whole phrases in capital letters should be avoided as these are hard to decipher given that the normal shape of the word has been obscured.
- Since the effort required to decode text impairs overall comprehension, some clients will fare better if text is read to them. They may need a helper to find the place when extracts from particular documents have to be located 'on the spot'.

When requesting information

- Take account of likely difficulty with recalling/reciting strings of numbers or letters (number plates, addresses, and so on).
- Be aware that, in a stressful situation, recall of times, places, and events may not be accurate. Comprehension will become increasingly impaired.

Additional Comments

- In many cases, rest breaks will be necessary to restore concentration (at least 10 minutes for every 50 minutes of the proceedings). Many people with specific learning difficulties will have reached 'mental overload' long before this.

- The stress and distractions of the court, together with the rapid 'cut and thrust' of questioning, disadvantage people with specific learning difficulties. Most would cope far better if they
  - were allowed to use a video link;
  - had a friend/'appropriate adult' to help them locate and digest documentation;
  - were encouraged to take their time in answering questions so that they could provide a thoughtful response.

> People with dyslexia, dyspraxia, and attention deficit (hyperactivity) disorder vary greatly in the difficulties they experience, and so accommodations need to be adapted to suit each individual.
>
> Do not make assumptions – individuals should be asked to state their own preferences.

Conclusion

Sylvia Moody

In this book, we have given information on good practice in workplace dyslexia consultancy and reflected on our own practice in this field: we have considered how we handled cases that presented particular challenges and also given some general perspectives on this area of work. From the rich and varied material presented in the book I shall draw out for discussion the following themes:

- Identifying dyslexia.
- Workplace Needs assessments.
- Reasonable adjustments.
- Dealing with disputes.
- Employment tribunals.

Identifying Dyslexia

As dyslexia professionals working in the area of workplace consultancy we need to be clear about our understanding of the term *dyslexia*, and about the criteria we use in the assessment of dyslexic difficulties.

Many 'definitions', including the one favoured by the British Psychological Society, are child oriented: they define dyslexia mainly in terms of poor phonology or poor word reading. Such definitions are often irrelevant in adult assessment. Many intellectually able adults who have had good schooling and/or help for their difficulties have compensated well for their weak phonology and are able to read words with

Dyslexia and Employment Edited by Sylvia Moody
© 2009 John Wiley & Sons, Ltd

relative ease. Their spelling, too, may not fall far below the average level for the general population. Such definitions also ignore the wide range of other difficulties which dyslexic adults experience – difficulties such as poor organizational skills which often cause far greater problems than does poor word reading once an adult enters higher education or the workplace.

In the introduction to this book (page 3), I gave a description of typical adult difficulties. In Chapter 1, I described the 'spiky' cognitive profile which characterizes dyslexia: high scores on tests of verbal reasoning and perceptual abilities, contrasted with low or relatively low scores on tests of short-term memory and visual processing. This spiky profile can occur at all IQ levels, but a particular difficulty arises when it occurs within a set of scores which are all low or below average. Technically speaking, such a profile can still be termed 'dyslexic', but it is questionable how useful it is to emphasize a pattern of dyslexic difficulties in the context of generally low abilities. The support needed by a person with such a profile usually goes beyond the normal range of dyslexia support.

As regards literacy abilities, it is harder to find a profile which can be called typically dyslexic. Some dyslexic people may have severe difficulty with basic skills, such as word reading and spelling; others may score well on tests of basic skills, but struggle with higher level skills such as reading comprehension and structuring written work. It is important, therefore, that an assessment includes tests of these higher level skills.

Even if the full range of tests is done, an incorrect diagnosis can result from assessor error. For example, the assessor may fail to take a full history (thereby possibly missing signs of dyspraxia or ADD (attention deficit disorder)), may go too fast for her client on some of the verbal tests, or may fail to pick up the effects of visual stress on reading performance.

Workplace Needs Assessments

At present only a minority of dyslexia experts have the skills and experience to provide detailed and comprehensive advice about the needs of a dyslexic employee and how these should be met.

Workplace Needs assessments are sometimes done by work psychologists or occupational psychologists, who, though able to give advice on general work organization and time management, do not necessarily have expertise in dyslexia. Thus, an individual dyslexia training programme may not be specified and there may be no specific recommendations about how the IT training can be delivered in a dyslexia-friendly manner.

Conversely, professional groups who are knowledgeable about dyslexia, for example, educational psychologists and dyslexia tutors, generally specialize in assessing students in higher education; they may have little or no experience of a workplace consultancy and the different demands which this makes.

Ideally, a Workplace Needs assessment should be done by a dyslexia expert who is familiar with the culture of the workplace. The assessor should be able to make a personal recommendation for a workplace skills trainer and an IT trainer, and these two trainers should ideally be in a position to work in a complementary way when they are both helping the same client.

This situation of having a workplace-savvy dyslexia expert who has close professional contact with dyslexia and IT trainers is an ideal which is rarely achieved at the moment. However, a number of private organizations are now making efforts to set up teams of relevant professionals and to offer a 'one-stop-shop' service to employers.

Reasonable Adjustments

If an employee is found to have difficulties – whether specific or more general – the employer has a legal obligation under the Disability Discrimination Act to make reasonable adjustments to take account of the difficulties.

As regards dyslexic employees, there is a wide range of adjustments that can be recommended as appropriate in each case (see Information point B). As to the effectiveness of support packages, there are no research studies as yet which have looked in detail at this, but there is a good deal of evidence from single case studies that a well-thought-out support package delivered in a dyslexia-friendly way can enable a dyslexic employee to operate at an acceptably efficient level.

Similar support can be put in place for a person whose difficulties are more general, but there are questions about whether in such cases a standard dyslexia support programme will be adequate (though here success rates depend very heavily on the nature of the job).

An employer will often seek a definite answer from the assessor about whether a support programme will bring about the desired improvement, but no definite answer will usually be forthcoming. Favourite assessor reply words are 'probably', 'possibly', and 'unlikely'. Usually the best course is to advise the employer to try out the training programme for a limited number of sessions, and, if it seems to be bringing about improvement, extend it.

It has been stressed by a number of authors in the book that it is not sufficient for an employer to make reasonable adjustments simply on an ad hoc basis, that is, reacting to requests or demands from a particular employee. Ideally an organization should have dyslexia-friendly policies in place at every stage of the employment process – this includes recruitment, performance, appraisal, training, promotion, and redundancy/dismissal.

Dealing with Disputes

As noted in Chapter 4, when there is disagreement about the 'reasonableness' of suggested adjustments, it is important for the consultant to take an impartial stance and not to appear to be acting either as an advocate for the dyslexic person or as the 'tool' of the employer.

The consultant may be under considerable pressure from both sides. The employer may protest that the suggested adjustments are too expensive or demand that the consultant state definitely that the recommended programme will produce the desired results.

On the other hand, the client may put pressure on the consultant by saying, for example, that if he (or she) is found not to be dyslexic, and is consequently denied support, he will lose his job and his life will be ruined. Occasionally a client will even threaten suicide.

As well as this, there are often a number of power games in progress in a workplace. Different managers or work colleagues may have agendas of their own which influence their view of a situation in which a dyslexic employee seeks help and support. Emotional factors could also play a role, sometimes in a surprising way: a manager may himself/herself have dyslexic difficulties which they have kept as a closely guarded 'guilty secret', and so may feel ambivalent about a junior colleague taking an assertive attitude to such difficulties. Or a dyslexic manager may, through fellow feeling, try to keep a dyslexic employee in a job even when it has become obvious that he/she is incapable of doing it.

The dyslexia consultant needs to try to reconcile different viewpoints and negotiate a solution which is acceptable to all parties. If these negotiations fail, then the matter may well go to an employment tribunal.

Employment Tribunals

When called to give evidence at an employment tribunal, a dyslexia consultant will, of course, take pains to be impartial, irrespective of whether he/she has been retained by the plaintiff or the defendant. He/she may in fact be asked to act as 'joint witness', that is, to be jointly retained by both sides in the dispute. At all events the expert witness is answerable to the Court, not to either of the disputants, and this responsibility is acknowledged in the courtroom by the fact that the expert witness always faces towards the judge when giving evidence. However, this does not prevent each side in a dispute exerting subtle – often unconscious – pressure on the expert to reach the conclusion each desires.

Another trap for the unwary expert is the 'solicitor's instructions', that is, the questions the solicitor asks the expert. These often contain a request that the expert state definitely that a dyslexic person, with suitable training, will or will not be able to do a particular job. More dauntingly the solicitor may ask whether, in the case of, say, a dyslexic firefighter, there are circumstances in which the firefighter's dyslexic difficulties might put life at risk.

The expert would be well advised to decline to answer such questions. He/she could point out that, in the field of adult dyslexia, it is not possible to quote statistics of probability, as it may be in medical cases. For example, a surgeon will be able to say what proportion of patients are cured by a particular operation, but a dyslexia expert has no such statistics available for the efficacy of tuition. As regards risk assessments for firefighters, nurses, and so on, such assessments are outside the professional expertise of a dyslexia assessor.

It is important, too, to keep in mind the difference between a professional *opinion* on a person's difficulties and a legal *judgement* on whether or not those difficulties amount to a disability. The dyslexia assessor's role is to give an opinion only, and the Court will take this opinion, along with other evidence, into account when making its judgement.

Finally, a more general point regarding legal proceedings: whenever a dyslexia consultant is called upon to act as an expert witness, it is important that, in the weeks of preparation before a tribunal or trial, the consultant should ensure that all the legal professionals involved in the case are aware of dyslexic difficulties, of how these might hamper a dyslexic person in police interviews and in giving evidence in court, and of what sort of accommodations should be made for them. (For detailed guidance on this, see Information point I.)

Endword

Perhaps one of the main messages that comes from all of the above is that nothing is ever quite definite in the dyslexia world. Dyslexia is a slippery character, a protean rascal who constantly eludes our grasp. The dyslexia consultant has to keep a steady nerve in the face of all the uncertainties: uncertainties about whether a person's difficulties are best described as dyslexic, about whether training will be effective, about whether adjustments are reasonable. Measles is measles, and that is an end of it, but with dyslexia, the arguing is never done . . . .

It is hoped that this book, if not providing definite answers, will have provided useful information and opened up discussion on a range of important issues. The world of workplace dyslexia consultancy is still in its infancy – its healthy development will depend on the care and thought which it receives in the coming years.

APPENDIX I

Checklists

Dyslexia Checklist

If you tick most of the items below, you could consider having an assessment with a dyslexia specialist.

(a) Workplace difficulties

	Tick if YES
Reading	
Following written instructions	☐
Following technical manuals	☐
Quickly getting gist of letters/reports, etc.	☐
Recalling what has been read	☐
Writing	
Confusing reversible letters, e.g., b, d	☐
Sequencing letters (discussion – dicsussion)	☐
Spelling	☐
Handwriting	☐
Filling in forms	☐

These checklists © Sylvia Moody, who grants permission for the checklists to be copied.

Expressing ideas clearly in writing .... ☐

Writing memos/letters.. ☐

Writing reports .... ☐

Taking notes/Minutes .... ☐

Numerical data

Copying numbers.. ☐

Tabulating numbers... ☐

Doing arithmetical calculations .... ☐

Using calculator.. ☐

Speech and comprehension

Following a conversation/discussion......................... ☐

Contributing to a discussion .... ☐

Presenting thoughts succinctly .... ☐

Memory and concentration

Following oral instructions .... ☐

Remembering: telephone numbers............................ ☐

messages .... ☐

appointments................................. ☐

Concentrating for long periods .... ☐

Visuomotor skills

Inputting data on computer/calculator........................ ☐

Analyzing complex visual arrays, e.g., maps, graphs, tables of figures .... ☐

Getting bearings in large or complex buildings.............. ☐

Sequencing

Filing .... ☐

Retrieving files .... ☐

Looking up entries in dictionaries/directories .... ☐

Organization

Planning work schedules .... ☐

Meeting deadlines .... ☐

Keeping papers in order .... ☐

Working efficiently .... ☐

(b) Everyday difficulties

Writing a cheque .... ☐

Filling in forms .... ☐

Writing letters .... ☐

Reading letters .... ☐

Reading official documents .... ☐

Reading a newspaper .... ☐

Understanding operating/safety instructions on household gadgets .. ☐

Reading television schedules .... ☐

Reading recipes .... ☐

Reading bus/train timetables .... ☐

Making shopping lists .... ☐

Dealing with money in shops .... ☐

Checking bank statements .... ☐

Keeping track of outstanding bills .... ☐

Explaining things clearly to others .... ☐

Placing orders over the telephone .... ☐

Conducting enquiries over the telephone	☐
Following spoken instructions	☐
Following left–right instructions	☐
Reading maps	☐
Reading signposts	☐
Orienting oneself in a strange place or complex environment, e.g., tube station	☐
Remembering where things have been put	☐
Looking up telephone numbers in directories	☐
Recording telephone numbers correctly	☐
Remembering messages	☐
Remembering appointments	☐
Organizing daily life	☐
Concentrating for longer than an hour	☐
Working continuously for longer than an hour	☐

(c) Dyspraxia

If you tick most of these items, you could consider having an assessment with a dyspraxia specialist.

	Tick if Yes
Do you bump into things/people and often trip over?	☐
Do you spill and drop things often?	☐

Do you find it difficult to do practical tasks such as: cooking .... ☐

DIY .... ☐

typing .... ☐

keying numbers on the phone. ☐

driving a car ... ☐

riding a bike ... ☐

Do you find sports difficult, especially team and bat and ball games? ☐

Do you find it difficult to judge distance and space? .... ☐

Are you over/under sensitive to: sound .... ☐

smell .... ☐

taste .... ☐

Are you generally disorganized and untidy? .... ☐

Do you have problems prioritizing and discriminating the essential from the inessential? .... ☐

Do you find it hard to finish off work? .... ☐

Do you often lose things and find it difficult to remember where you have put them? .... ☐

Do you have problems working against a background of noise? ..... ☐

Is there a delay between hearing something and understanding it? ... ☐

Do you take spoken and written words literally and find it hard to pick up shades of meaning? .... ☐

Do you find it difficult to interpret body language? .... ☐

Do you interrupt people often? .... ☐

(d) Visual stress

If you tick most of these items, you could consider having an assessment with an optometrist who specializes in colorimetry.
Items 1, 2, 3, 5, 6, 15, and 17 are very common indicators of visual stress.

	Tick if Yes
1. Does reading make you tired?	☐
2. Do you often lose your place when reading?	☐
3. Do you reread or skip lines when reading?	☐
4. Do you read words/numbers back to front?	☐
5. Do you miss out or misread words when reading?	☐
6. Do you use a marker or your finger to keep the place?	☐
7. Are you easily distracted when reading?	☐
8. Do you become restless or fidgety when reading?	☐
9. Do you get headaches when you read?	☐
10. Do your eyes become sore or water?	☐
11. Do you screw your eyes up when reading?	☐
12. Do you rub or close one eye when reading?	☐
13. Do your difficulties increase the longer you read?	☐
14. Do you prefer dim light to bright light for reading?	☐
15. Does white paper (or white board) seem to glare?	☐
16. Does print seem to move about as you read?	☐
17. Does print become distorted or shimmer as you read?	☐
18. Do you find striped patterns uncomfortable to look at?	☐
19. Is it uncomfortable to read under fluorescent lighting?	☐

This checklist © Melanie Jameson, who grants permission for the checklist to be copied.

APPENDIX II

Assistive Technology

In this appendix, you will find *general* information on IT and general technological support for people with dyslexic difficulties. For advice on *specific* items of hardware or software packages that would suit your particular requirements, consult a specialist in the field (see Appendix III, page 234). Try to get a hands-on demonstration or a free trial of software before purchasing anything.

Note that price is not always an indicator of usefulness, and also that most AT software is designed for PCs, not Macs.

You may be able to apply for VAT relief on certain items. For advice on this contact: advice@dyslexic.com 01223 420101

Organization

Personal digital assistants (PDAs) are hand-held organizers that work like mini-computers. They can store your diary, set alarmed reminders for appointments, create 'to do' lists, store pictures, record notes and messages, and store documents for reading and editing wherever you are. You can synchronize your PDA with your desktop PC or laptop to keep your diary and contacts list up to date. Also available are sub notebooks with 7" screens.

There are also some useful organizational tools available within Microsoft Office – for example, Microsoft Outlook has a simple-to-use

Dyslexia and Employment Edited by Sylvia Moody
© 2009 John Wiley & Sons, Ltd

calendar/diary function as well as contact lists, task lists, memos, and systems for organizing e-mails.

Also, mind-mapping software such as 'Inspiration Idea Organizer', 'Mind Manager', and 'Mind Genius' are powerful organizational and memory tools.

Speech Recognition

There are software packages that allow you to dictate into your computer and have the written word appear on the screen. The text can then be edited and printed, using, for example, Microsoft Word. The software also has the ability to 'transcribe' voice recordings from digital recorders and PDAs.

Caution: Speech-recognition software is trained to understand *your* voice, so it will *not* be able to transcribe recordings of talks and meetings.

Reading: Text-to-Speech Software

Text-to-speech programmes can read out loud practically any text that is on the screen. They help you to concentrate on what you are reading and to absorb the meaning of a text more easily. You can also use the software to read back what you yourself have written and this helps with proofreading.

Scanning

Optical character recognition software can scan printed documents and convert them into text documents on your computer. You can then read the documents on your computer screen in the colour and format that suits you best: perhaps in larger print, with double spacing, or using different coloured backgrounds and print. Or use text-to-speech software to have the documents read aloud to you.

Caution: Scanning whole books or large amounts of text is laborious and usually not worth the effort.

Notetaking

You can use a digital voice recorder to 'jot down' notes and reminders to yourself, which can then be played back or transcribed into a text document on your computer using speech-recognition software. The recorder can also be used to record talks and meetings for playing back at a later time, reducing the need to take handwritten notes. Recording efficiency varies according to the acoustic environment. It is usually preferable to use an external microphone.

Caution: Make sure you choose a recorder that has a long recording time and PC connectivity.

Audio Notetaker is a software package which helps with navigating, annotating, and organizing digital recordings. It enables you to see a visual representation of what you are listening to, and to later identify, review, and reference key sections of it, thus making voice recordings more accessible and more productive.

Typing Tutors

Being able to type confidently, accurately, and quickly will free your mind to concentrate on the content of what you are typing. There are several computer-interactive typing tutors that will give you training in touch typing.

Spelling

Make sure you are making the best use of the spell checkers that come as standard within, for example, Microsoft Office. There are also sophisticated add-ons to word-processing packages that offer phonetic and homophone spell checkers, word prediction, and subject-specific spell checkers, for example, for medicine. Hand-held spell checkers with similar add-ons are also available.

Writing

You can plan and structure reports and other documents using computer-generated 'spider maps' and flow charts. At the click of your mouse these maps can be converted into text and exported to your preferred word-processing package, presentation software (such as PowerPoint), or other software packages. You can then edit the text using the keyboard or voice-recognition software, and finally proof it with the help of a screen reader.

Giving Talks/Presentations

Check if your employer can provide an 'interactive' whiteboard, linked to a computer. You can then

- write on the screen to highlight and annotate points in documents and presentations;
- view and navigate the Internet and display web sites that your whole audience will be able to see;
- project movie files and DVDs onto a large screen;
- allow members of the audience to add their contributions to word-processed documents, spreadsheets, and so on, by writing directly onto them;
- save information for printing as handout notes, or uploading onto the Internet/Intranet.

Whiteboard 'glare' can be avoided by changing the colours projected onto the screen through the computer's Windows properties/appearance function.

Colour Sensitivity

Microsoft Windows operating systems allow customization of your computer with tools designed to help users with disabilities. For example, changing screen and font colours can reduce eye strain and prevent text from 'swimming' on the page. These functions are, however, limited, and you may prefer to buy a specialized piece of software that can change all Windows colours, including the background colour, default text colour, menu background, text colour, and toolbars. Similar software for web pages is also available.

When reading books or papers, you could use coloured overlays or reading rulers to stabilize the words. Professional overlays are available from Cerium Visual Technologies; and eye-level coloured reading rulers are available from Crossbow Education (see page 235).

A screen filter reduces glare from the computer screen and aids visual processing.

Screen Rulers

If you have difficulty keeping your place on the screen, a screen ruler could be helpful. Acting as an 'overlay' on the screen, it creates a ruler that can be moved up and down with the mouse. Some versions can dim out areas of the screen that are not in use.

Route Planning and Navigation Systems

Route planners are computer programmes displaying street maps and road networks throughout the United Kingdom and abroad. They enable you to plot the route to your destination, and can be can be accessed through a web site, your desktop PC, laptop, or PDA. Some systems let you print out maps of the proposed route as well as directions, such as when to take a turn.

Navigation aids are linked to the global positioning system, which uses satellites to locate your position anywhere in the world to within a few metres. The software can direct you along a route as you travel.

Caution: Take care to choose the style of interface that suits you best. Some people prefer detailed maps, others simple directional arrows.

Portable Data Storage

You can copy your files onto a USB storage device (not much larger than your thumb) and carry them around with you. To access your data, simply plug the device into the USB port on another PC.

Good Working Practices

Choose a chair that supports your back; do not slump on a couch or work with a laptop on your knee.

Do not sit too close to the screen. If possible, have the screen at right angles to the light source.

If you find that working on a laptop causes strain or discomfort, consider buying an external full-sized keyboard and screen and a wireless mouse. An ergonomic keyboard (designed for comfort and ease of use) is a wise investment as it encourages good posture. Dyspraxic people, in particular, find this type of keyboard helpful. Also useful: wrist rests and mouse pads with wrist support.

Buying Hardware and Software – General Advice

If you already own a computer, do not purchase any software until you have checked with the supplier that it is compatible with your equipment.

Specialist software is not widely available in high street stores, but it can usually be purchased over the Internet. Before buying anything, get up-to-date advice on all your hardware and software requirements.

APPENDIX III

Useful Addresses

Advice Organizations

Bangor Dyslexia Unit
University of Wales, Gwynedd LL57 2DG
Tel: 01248 382 203
E-mail: dyslex-admin@bangor.ac.uk
Web site: www.dyslexia.bangor.ac.uk
This branch covers the whole of Wales.

British Dyslexia Association (BDA)
Unit 8, Bracknell Beeches, Old Bracknell Lane, Bracknell RG12 7BW
Tel: 0845 251 9002
E-mail: helpline@bdadyslexia.org.uk
Web site: www.bdadyslexia.org.uk
For list of all local associations, click on Information.

Dyslexia Association of Ireland
Suffolk Chambers, 1 Suffolk Street, Dublin 2
Tel: 01 679 0276
E-mail: info@dyslexia-ie
Web site: www.dyslexia.ie

© 2009 John Wiley & Sons, Ltd

Dyslexia Scotland
Stirling Business Centre, Wellgreen, Stirling FK8 2DZ
Tel: 01786 446650
E-mail: info@dyslexiascotland.org.uk
Web site: www.dyslexiascotland.org.uk

Dyslexia Parents Resource
Web site: www.dyslexia-parent.com
Gives contact details for all BDA local associations.

European Dyslexia Association
Web site: www.dyslexia.eu.com

International Dyslexia Association
Web site: www.interdys.org

Workplace Dyslexia Specialists

Adult Dyslexia Service
61 Woodland Rise
London N10 3UN
Tel: 020 8444 0851
E-mail: brends@bjallan.co.uk

Dyslexia Advice and Training Services
33 South Grove House, South Grove, London N6 6LR
Tel: 020 8348 7110
E-mail: bhdyslexia@yahoo.co.uk

Dyslexia Assessment and Consultancy
41 Cardigan Street, Kennington, London SE11 5PF
Tel: 020 7582 6117
Fax: 020 7587 0546
E-mail: info@workingwithdyslexia.com
Web site: www.workingwithdyslexia.com

Dyslexia Assessment Service
22 Wray Crescent, London N4 3LP
Tel: 020 7272 6429

Dyslexia Consultancy
6 Gilbert Road, Malvern, Worcs. WR14 3RQ
Tel: 01684 572 466
E-mail: dyslexia.mj@dsl.pipex.com

Fitzgibbon Associates
39-41 North Road, London N7 9DP
Tel: 0845 111 6543
E-mail: fae@fitzgibbonassociates.co.uk

Independent Dyslexia Consultants
2nd Floor, 1-7 Woburn Walk, London WC1H OJJ
Tel: 020 7388 8744
E-mail: info@dyslexia-idc.org
Web site: www.adultdyslexiacentre.co.uk

Key4Learning
The Old Village Stores, Chedworth, Cheltenham, Gloucester GL54 4AA
Tel: 01285 720 964
E-mail: enquiries@key4learning.com
Web site: www.key4learning.com

Workplace Needs Assessment only:
Access to Work Operational Units.
Contact directory enquiries for local Unit, or ask at your local JobCentrePlus.

Careers Advice

Careers Advice for Dyslexic Adults
33 South Grove House, South Grove, London N6 6LR
Tel: 020 8348 7110
E-mail: bhdyslexia@yahoo.co.uk

Training Days for Managers and Dyslexia Professionals

Dyslexia Assessment and Consultancy
41 Cardigan Street, Kennington, London SE11 5PF
Tel: 020 7582 6117
Fax: 020 7587 0546
E-mail: info@workingwithdyslexia.com
Web site: www.workingwithdyslexia.com

Workplace Advice

Dyslexia Adults link
Web site: www.dyslexia-adults.com
Offers general advice for adult dyslexics and has an extensive section on workplace difficulties.

JobCentrePlus
Web site: www.jobcentreplus.gov.uk
Offers advice on coping with disability in the workplace.

General Dyslexia Assessment and Tuition

It is important that assessment and tuition are carried out by chartered psychologists or tutors who are dyslexia specialists and have experience in working with adults. Consult your local branch of the British Dyslexia Association (see above) or Dyslexia Action (see below) for advice.

Dyslexia Action
Park House, Wick Road, Egham, Surrey TW20 0HH
Tel: 01784 222 300
E-mail: info@dyslexiaaction.org.uk
Web site: www.dyslexiaaction.org.uk

Dyslexia Teaching Centre
23 Kensington Square, London W8 5HN
Tel: 020 7361 4790
E-mail: dyslexiateacher@tiscali.co.uk
Web site: www.dyslexia-teaching-centre.org.uk

Helen Arkell Dyslexia Centre
Frensham, Farnham, Surrey GU10 3BW
Tel: 01252 792 400
E-mail: enquiries@arkellcentre.org.uk
Web site: www.arkellcentre.org.uk
Covers Surrey, Hampshire, Southwest London.

London Dyslexia Action
2 Grosvenor Gardens, London SW1W 0DH
Tel: 020 7730 8890
E-mail: london@dyslexiaaction.org.uk
Web site: www.dyslexiaaction.org.uk

PATOSS (dyslexia tutors organization)
PO Box 10, Evesham, Worcestershire WR11 1ZW
Tel: 01386 712650
E-mail: patoss@evesham.ac.uk
Web site: www.patoss-dyslexia.org

Tuition for Dyslexic Adults
20a Pymmes Green Road
London N11 1BY
Tel: 020 8368 3634
E-mail: dianabart@aol.com

Audio Libraries

Among the audio libraries that offer a mail-order service are:

Calibre
Web site: www.calibre.org.uk

Listening Books
Web site: www.listening-books.org.uk

Dyspraxia Support

Developmental Adult Neuro-Diversity Association (DANDA)
46 Westbere Road, London NW2 3RU
Tel: 020 7435 7891
E-mail: mary.colley@danda.org.uk
Web site: www.danda.org.uk

Dyscovery Centre
Alltyryn Campus, University of Wales, Newport NP20 5DA
Tel: 01633 432 330
E-mail: dyscoverycentre@newport.ac.uk
Web site: www.dyscovery.co.uk

Dyspraxia Association of Ireland
69a Main Street, Leixlip, Co Kildare
Tel: 01 295 7125
E-mail: info@dyspraxiaireland.com
Web site: www.dyspraxiaireland.com

Dyspraxia Foundation
8 West Alley, Hitchin, Herts SG5 1EG
Tel: 01462 454 986
E-mail: dyspraxia@dyspraxiafoundation.org.uk
Web site: www.dyspraxiafoundation.org.uk

Dyspraxia Connections
21 Birchdale Avenue, Hucknall, Notts NG15 6DL
Tel: 0115 963 2220
Web site: www.dyspraxiaconnexion.org.uk

IT Advice and Training

AbilityNet
PO Box 94, Warwick CV34 5WS
Tel: 01926 312847 or 0800 269545 (helpline freephone)
E-mail: enquiries@abilitynet.org.uk
Web site: www.abilitynet.org.uk

Dyslexia in the Workplace
Flat 2, Grafton Chambers, Churchway, London NW1 1LN
Tel: 020 7388 3807
E-mail: workplacedyslexia@btopenworld.com

Iansyst Ltd
Fen House, Fen Road, Cambridge CB4 1UN
Tel: 01223 420101
E-mail: advice@dyslexic.com
Web site: www.dyslexic.com
To find a local consultant, check with your local branch of the British Dyslexia Association (see above).

Visual Problems

Colorimetry assessments for visual stress are not done in standard eye tests; contact the Dyslexia Research Trust or Cerium Visual Technologies (below) for a specialist in your area.

Barnard Levit Associates
58 Clifton Gardens, London NW11 7EL
Tel: 020 8458 0599
E-mail: reception@eye-spy.co.uk

Cerium Visual Technologies
Cerium Technology Park, Tenterden, Kent TN30 7DE
Tel: 01580 765 211
E-mail: CeriumUK@ceriumvistech.co.uk
Web site: www.ceriumvistech.co.uk
Sells tinted overlays.

Crossbow Education
41 Sawpit Lane, Brocton, Stafford, ST17 0TE
Tel: 01785 660902
E-mail: sales@crossboweducation.com
Web site: www.crossboweducation.com
Sells eye-level coloured reading rulers.

Dyslexia Research Trust
University Laboratory of Physiology, Parks Road, Oxford OX1 3PT
Tel: 01865 272 116
E-mail: info@dyslexic.org.uk
Web site: www.dyslexic.org.uk

Institute of Optometry
56–62 Newington Causeway, London SE1 6DS
Tel: 020 7234 9641
E-mail: admin@ioo.org.uk
Web site: www.ioo.org.uk

Legal Advice

Equality and Human Rights Commission
Tel: 08457 622 633
Web site: www.equalityhumanrights.com

Legal Services Commission
Web site: www.legalservices.gov.uk www.clsdirect.org.uk

Law Centres
Web site: www.lawcentres.org.uk

Disability Law Service
Web site: www.dls.org.uk

Office of Public Sector Information
Web site: www.opsi.gov.uk
Type 'Disability Discrimination Act' into the 'search' window to read the relevant sections of the Act in full.

General Counselling

British Association of Counselling
BACP House, 15 St Johns' Business Park, Lutterworth, Leics LE17 4HB
Tel: 0870 443 5252
E-mail: bacp@bacp.co.uk
Web site: www.bacp.co.uk
GP surgeries sometimes have counsellors. Also your local *council* or your local *radio helpdesk* may have details of local counselling organizations.

Further and Higher Education

SKILL: National Bureau for Students with Disabilities
Chapter House, 18-20 Crucifix Lane, London SEI 3JW
Tel: 020 7450 0620
E-mail: skill@skill.org.uk
Web site: www.skill.org.uk

World of Dyslexia Ltd
Web site: www.dyslexia-college.com
Offers useful information on topics from reading techniques to applying for grants.

APPENDIX IV

Further Reading

Books

Workplace

Bartlett, D. and Moody, S. (2000) *Dyslexia in the Workplace*, Wiley.

Jargon-free guide for dyslexic workers, employers, and dyslexia professionals

Reid, G. and Kirk, J. (2001) *Dyslexia in Adults: Education and Employment*, Wiley.

For dyslexia professionals

Fitzgibbon, G. and O'Connor, B. (2002) *Adult Dyslexia: A Guide for the Workplace*, Wiley.

For occupational psychologists, employers, and dyslexia professionals

Moody, S. (2006) *Dyslexia: How to Survive and Succeed at Work*, Random House (Vermilion).

Practical self-help manual for dyslexic workers, and guidance for employers

Hagan, B. et al. (ed.)(2007) *British Dyslexia Association Code of Practice: Employers*.

Legal

Hall, J.G. (2006) *The Expert Witness*, Barry Rose Law Publishers Limited.

© 2009 John Wiley & Sons, Ltd

Education

Moody, S. (2007) Dyslexia: Surviving and Succeding at College, Routledge.

General interest

Grant, D. (2005) *That's the Way I Think: Dyslexia and Dyspraxia Explained*, David Fulton.

Miles, T. (ed.) (2004) *Dyslexia and Stress*, Wiley.

McLoughlin, D., Leather, C. and Stringer, P. (2002) *The Adult Dyslexic: Interventions and Outcomes*, Wiley.

Morgan, E. and Klein, C. (2000) *The Dyslexic Adult in a Non-Dyslexic World*, Wiley.

Dyspraxia

Colley, M. (2006) *Living with Dyspraxia*, Jessica Kingsley.

Pamphlets

Briefing Paper 6 on Dyslexia in the Workplace. Available from: Employers Forum on Disability, www.employers-forum.co.uk.

Hagan, B. *Dyslexia in the Workplace: A Guide for Unions*, TUC, www.tuc.org.uk/publications.

Articles

Workplace

Bartlett, D. and Moody, S. (2000a) Assessing and managing developmental dyslexia in the workplace. *Journal of the Application of Occupational Psychology to Employment and Disability*, **2** (2), 27–35.

Close, S. (2006) Dyslexia and technological aids in the workplace. *PATOSS Bulletin*, **19** (1), 65–8.

Hagan, B. (2006) Fighting discrimination in the workplace. *The Dyslexia Handbook*, 217–37.

Kindersley, K. (2007) Support for adults with dyslexia through Access to Work. *PATOSS Bulletin*, **20** (1), 68–70.

Moody, S. (2003) Dyslexia in the workplace: assessment and training. *Dyslexia Review*, **14** (2), 16–7.

Moody, S. (2005) Workplace needs assessments and expert witness work. *PATOSS Bulletin*, **18** (2), 33–8.

Moody, S. (2007a) Writing reports for Access to Work. *PATOSS Bulletin*, **20** (2), 45–9.
Moody, S. (2007b) Dyslexia: three types of assessment. *The Dyslexia Handbook*, 189–94.
Moody, S. (2009) Workplace needs assessments: how to arrange and apprise them. *The Dyslexia Employment Handbook.*
Moody, S. (2009) Dyslexia on the Defensive. *The Dyslexia Handbook.*

Legal

Moody, S. (2001a) Dyslexia and the Disability Discrimination Act: a solicitor's guide. *Medical Litigation*, **3**, 11–2.
Moody, S. (2001b) Dyslexia in the dock. *Dyslexia Review*, **13** (1), 8–10.
Moody, S. (2001c) Dyslexia and the Disability Discrimination Act. *Employment Lawyers Association Briefing*, **8**, 12.

Author Biographies

Brenda Allan is the director of the Adult Dyslexia Service in London, an assessment and advisory service for adults in education or employment, and for employers. She provides training for employers and assessors on dyslexia assessment. She also works as a consultant, designing and evaluating outcomes in mental health services, and on staff recruitment and development issues.

Diana Bartlett is a psychologist, specializing in language, learning, dyslexia, and memory. She works as a one-to-one trainer and adviser for dyslexic adults in the workplace and in education. She is co-author, with Sylvia Moody, of the book *Dyslexia in the Workplace*.

David Grant is a Chartered Psychologist and writer who specializes in diagnosing adults with specific learning differences. His work has been published in a number of journals, including Personnel Management. His recent publications include '*That's the Way I Think: Dyslexia and Dyspraxia Explained*', and a commissioned handbook on Neurodiversity for members of the National Association of Disability Practitioners.

Brian Hagan was formerly a senior HR manager and Management Consultant, and is now director of Dyslexia Advice and Training Services, in London. He specializes in advising employers on reasonable adjustments and in delivering related skills training for dyslexic employees; he also offers a careers advice service to dyslexic adults. He

Dyslexia and Employment Edited by Sylvia Moody
© 2009 John Wiley & Sons, Ltd

has written and contributed to publications on dyslexia for people in employment and their advisors.

Sarah Howard is an assessor and tutor who specializes in supporting and training dyslexic and dyspraxic adults. She works with students in higher education and with people in employment, as well as advising HR and line managers, unions, and other workplace organizations.

Melanie Jameson of Dyslexia Consultancy Malvern, has produced a wide range of dyslexia training materials, guides, and information sheets as well as guidelines for government departments. She has a special interest in disseminating awareness of dyslexia amongst professionals within the justice system and is Special Adviser to the Developmental Adult Neuro-Diversity Association (DANDA).

Katherine Kindersley is the director of Dyslexia Assessment and Consultancy, an organization which works with private and public companies, government organizations, as well as individuals, providing assessment, training, and advice on reasonable adjustments. She runs regular training courses for dyslexia professionals on employment consultancy work, and for managers on dyslexia awareness. She is also experienced in doing legal assessments and expert witness work.

Sylvia Moody is a clinical psychologist and psychotherapist specializing in the assessment of dyslexic adults. She is the director of the Dyslexia Assessment Service in London and has written books on dyslexia for teenagers, college students, and people in employment.

Pauline Sumner is a senior lecturer and dyslexia support tutor at Middlesex University. Her work involves work placement dyslexia support in nursing, midwifery, and teaching. She produces instructional/training resources including web-based materials for dyslexic students and workplace mentors, and provides dyslexia training and support in the workplace.